W9-BKK-577

DATE DUE

NOV 2 0 1996		
MAR 2 2 2016		

DEMCO 38-297

The
EVOLUTION
of the
AIRLINE
INDUSTRY

The
EVOLUTION
of the
AIRLINE
INDUSTRY

Steven A. Morrison and
Clifford Winston

THE BROOKINGS INSTITUTION
Washington, D.C.

Library of Congress Cataloging-in-Publication Data

Morrison, Steven, 1951–
    The evolution of the airline industry / Steven A. Morrison,
Clifford Winston.
        p. cm.
    Includes index.
    Contents: Introduction—Profile of the airline industry—
Organizational and methodological overview—Carrier behavior and
traveler welfare—Airline profitability—Industry evolution—
Summary and policy implications.
    ISBN 0-8157-5844-8.—ISBN 0-8157-5843-X (pbk.)
    1. Airlines—United States—History. 2. Aeronautics, Commercial—
United States—History.   I. Winston, Clifford, 1952–
II. Title.
HE9803.A3M67   1995
387.7'0973—dc20   95-4435
                                                                        CIP

9 8 7 6 5 4 3 2 1

The paper used in this publication meets the minimum
requirements of the American National Standard for Information
Sciences—Permanence of Paper for Printed Library Materials,
ANSI Z39.48-1984.

Typeset in Times Roman

Composition by Harlowe Typography Inc.,
Cottage City, Maryland

Printed by R. R. Donnelley and Sons Co.
Harrisonburg, Virginia

₿ THE BROOKINGS INSTITUTION

The Brookings Institution is an independent organization devoted to nonpartisan research, education, and publication in economics, government, foreign policy, and the social sciences generally. Its principal purposes are to aid in the development of sound public policies and to promote public understanding of issues of national importance.

The Institution was founded on December 8, 1927, to merge the activities of the Institute for Government Research, founded in 1916, the Institute of Economics, founded in 1922, and the Robert Brookings Graduate School of Economics and Government, founded in 1924.

The Board of Trustees is responsible for the general administration of the Institution, while the immediate direction of the policies, program, and staff is vested in the President, assisted by an advisory committee of the officers and staff. The by-laws of the Institution state: "It is the function of the Trustees to make possible the conduct of scientific research, and publication, under the most favorable conditions, and to safeguard the independence of the research staff in the pursuit of their studies and in the publication of the results of such studies. It is not a part of their function to determine, control, or influence the conduct of particular investigations or the conclusions reached."

The President bears final responsibility for the decision to publish a manuscript as a Brookings book. In reaching his judgment on the competence, accuracy, and objectivity of each study, the President is advised by the director of the appropriate research program and weighs the views of a panel of expert outside readers who report to him in confidence on the quality of the work. Publication of a work signifies that it is deemed a competent treatment worthy of public consideration but does not imply endorsement of conclusions or recommendations.

The Institution maintains its position of neutrality on issues of public policy in order to safeguard the intellectual freedom of the staff. Hence interpretations or conclusions in Brookings publications should be understood to be solely those of the authors and should not be attributed to the Institution, to its trustees, officers, or other staff members, or to the organizations that support its research.

Foreword

BECAUSE THE U.S. airline industry was one of the first industries to be fully deregulated, its performance has continued to be of considerable interest to policymakers and analysts. This interest has been compounded by dramatic changes in airfares and service, a continual shifting of carrier strategies to increase market share, and sharp fluctuations in earnings that have helped send three airlines into liquidation in the past ten years.

In this study Steven A. Morrison and Clifford Winston assess the evolution of the industry and discuss whether government policy can help improve airline performance. They consider travel time, pricing, scheduling, and related matters with a focus on the extent to which deregulation has improved customer welfare. The authors conclude that, despite fits and starts, the evolution of the industry is proceeding in a direction that will preserve and possibly enhance the benefits of deregulation for both travelers and carriers. They recommend that the federal government's primary policy in these matters should be to expand deregulation to include international travel.

The authors are grateful to Kenneth A. Small and Timothy Taylor for their thorough and constructive comments and to Alfred E. Kahn and John R. Meyer for their guidance and encouragement at various stages of the research. They have also received useful comments from Henry J. Aaron, George Borts, Barry P. Bosworth, Menzie D. Chinn, Robert W. Crandall, Kamran Dadkhah, John Kwoka, Don Pickrell, James Ratner, Philip A. Viton, and seminar participants at Harvard University, the Massachusetts Institute of Technology, the University of Chicago, the University of Maryland, and the U.S. Department of Justice.

Research assistance was provided by Sanjay Sarathy and Chad Shirley. James Schneider and Brenda Szittya edited the manuscript, David Bearce verified its factual content, and David Rossetti and Anita Whitlock provided staff assistance. Carlotta Ribar proofread the pages and Julia Petrakis compiled the index.

The views expressed in this book are those of the authors and should not be ascribed to those persons or organizations whose assistance is acknowledged or to the trustees, officers, or other staff members of the Brookings Institution.

BRUCE K. MACLAURY
President

August 1995
Washington, D.C.

Contents

Tables

Figures

PART ONE

Overview

CHAPTER ONE

Introduction

Is COMPETITION among airlines sufficient to ensure that passengers do not pay excessive fares? Can an unregulated airline industry be profitable? Is air travel safe? These questions, in various combinations, have been at the heart of debates about the airline industry very nearly from its beginning.

In 1914 passengers paid $5.00 to take America's first commercial plane flight, an eighteen-mile run of the St. Petersburg-Tampa Airboat Line.[1] The event was not a matter that concerned the U.S. government—not the airline, not the fare, not the route, not the safety of passengers. But within only twelve years that was to change. It did not happen the way one might expect. To speed mail delivery nationwide, in 1926 the postmaster general began granting route authority to airlines based on their bids to provide airmail service. By 1927 the Post Office Department had contracted out all airmail service to private carriers, and government regulation of the fledgling airline industry had begun. Because passenger service was not initially feasible without a mail contract, subsidized service began with the postmaster general as the regulator of commercial air transport.

During the early 1930s Postmaster General Walter Brown sought to develop a national air transportation system. Apparently, he went too far, because in 1934 government investigators charged him and executives from the newly created big four airlines—American, Eastern, United, and Trans World—with colluding to monopolize the nation's airways, and President Roosevelt rescinded their airmail route authority. Although they eventually regained the right to fly the mail, they suffered severe financial losses during the time they operated without government contracts. By the time any carrier started to show a profit, the entire industry had been brought under regulation. The 1938 Civil Aeronautics Act was to regulate air fares and routes with a heavy hand for the next forty years.

1. Discussion of the history of the industry in this chapter is primarily drawn from R. E. G. Davies, *Airlines of the United States since 1914* (London: Putnam, 1972).

3

Enactment in 1978 of the Airline Deregulation Act breathed new life into discussions about whether the industry could be competitive and profitable. In the ensuing seventeen years, carriers' earnings have fluctuated wildly. Since 1989, several have gone bankrupt and Eastern, Braniff, Pan American, and Midway have been liquidated. Concerns have also arisen that service has deteriorated and safety is being compromised by carriers who cut costs by skimping on maintenance and hiring inexperienced pilots.

Indeed, although the controversial issues concerning air transportation have remained essentially the same over the years, the intensity of the debate has sharply increased with the advent of deregulation. Economic regulation provided a certain stability for both passengers and the industry: fares were predictable and uniform, carriers' earnings fluctuated but bankruptcies were averted through mergers sanctioned by the Civil Aeronautics Board, and air safety steadily improved.[2] Deregulation changed everything. A new fare structure took shape. Travelers faced a variety of fares and concomitant travel restrictions. And the offerings changed frequently. New carriers entered the industry, but nearly as many left, often through merger, or continued to operate while in bankruptcy. As financial pressures mounted, safety practices came into question. Many critics called for a return to some form of regulation.

Much of what has been written about the airline industry and deregulation has focused on the industry's performance at a particular time.[3] These analyses have provided estimates of the effects of deregulation on travelers and carriers, described but rarely quantified the implications of some important airline practices and operations that have developed since deregulation, and studied the relation between fares and changes in competition on different types of routes. This research, however, has

2. Economic regulations were initially enforced by the Civil Aeronautics Authority. They were taken over by the CAB in 1940.

3. Previous comprehensive studies and overviews of the industry include Elizabeth E. Bailey, David R. Graham, and Daniel P. Kaplan, *Deregulating the Airlines* (MIT Press, 1985); Steven Morrison and Clifford Winston, *The Economic Effects of Airline Deregulation* (Brookings, 1986); Michael E. Levine, "Airline Competition in Deregulated Markets: Theory, Firm Strategy, and Public Policy," *Yale Journal on Regulation*, vol. 4 (Spring 1987), pp. 393–494; John R. Meyer and Clinton V. Oster, Jr., *Deregulation and the Future of Intercity Passenger Travel* (MIT Press, 1987); Alfred E. Kahn, "Deregulation: Looking Backward and Looking Forward," *Yale Journal on Regulation*, vol. 7 (Summer 1990), pp. 325–54; Theodore E. Keeler, "Airline Deregulation and Market Performance: The Economic Basis for Regulatory Reform and Lessons from the U.S. Experience," in David Bannister and Kenneth J. Button, eds., *Transport in a Free Market Economy* (Macmillan, 1991); and Severin Borenstein, "The Evolution of U.S. Airline Competition," *Journal of Economic Perspectives*, vol. 6 (Spring 1992), pp. 45–73. A recent popular discussion is Paul Sheehan, "What Went Right," *Atlantic*, August 1993, pp. 82–88.

been conducted at a time when carriers have continued to search for effective strategies in the deregulated environment while rejecting those experiments that have failed. As such, some questions that have been raised before need to be evaluated over a longer time, important new matters that require quantitative analysis have emerged, and issues that may be important in the future need to be identified. In short, the evolution and likely direction of the industry need to be assessed.

That is the purpose of this book. We proceed by providing a comprehensive empirical profile of the industry as it has evolved both before and since deregulation. Armed with the facts and their implications, we identify the central issues facing travelers and carriers and assess their severity and underlying causes. We then develop a basis for understanding the industry's evolution and the ways it may eventually adapt to the unregulated economic environment. Finally, we discuss whether government policy can play an effective role in improving airline performance.

In the analysis that follows, we conclude that the evolution of the airline industry, despite fits and starts, is proceeding in a direction that will preserve and possibly enhance the benefits of deregulation for travelers and carriers. Indeed, the federal government's primary policy in these matters should be to expand deregulation to include international travel.

CHAPTER TWO

A Profile of the Airline Industry

OVER THE YEARS, government agencies, airline industry officials, and survey research firms have amassed data that represent the collective experience of the traveling public and the airline industry. This information is used in this book in two ways. In later chapters it provides the basis for analytical models of traveler and carrier behavior. In this chapter the raw but easily interpreted data provide a factual profile of industry competitiveness, fares, service quality, safety, and profits as they have evolved before and since deregulation. We examine these facts and their implications to assess the effects of deregulation. This kind of scrutiny provides an accurate picture of the deregulated airline industry and fosters the identification and discussion of the most crucial matters: How successful has deregulation been? In what sense—lower fares, more frequent service, more direct flights? And for whom—the airlines, the public, the nation at large? This scrutiny will also help us identify the controversies that still exist.

Between 1926, the first year the government compiled data on the fledgling industry, and 1993 the industry grew from 6,000 passengers flying 1 million passenger miles a year—and paying a dollar a mile (in 1993 dollars) for the speedy but cramped new service—to nearly half a billion passengers flying nearly a half trillion passenger miles for thirteen cents a mile (table 2-1). Although the economic slowdown of the early 1990s caused real passenger revenues and numbers of employees to decline from their 1990 highs, enplanements and passenger miles have continued to increase. Everyone agrees that the industry has continued to grow since deregulation.[1] The question is whether deregulation has improved the industry.

1. In this book, we use October 1978, the date the actual deregulation legislation was signed into law, as the start of deregulation. Because administrative deregulation began, however, with John Robson's appointment as Civil Aeronautics Board chairman in 1975 and continued with Alfred Kahn's tenure, we indicate throughout the book how certain

Table 2-1.   *U.S. Scheduled Airline Enplanements, Passenger Miles, Revenues, and Employees, Selected Years, 1926–93*

Year	Enplanements (thousands)	Passenger miles (millions)	Passenger revenue (millions of 1993 dollars)	Employees
1926	6	1	1	462[a]
1930	418	93	61	3,475
1940	2,966	1,152	641	22,051
1950	19,220	10,243	3,646	86,057
1960	57,872	38,863	11,657	167,603
1970	169,922	131,710	28,404	297,374
1975	205,062	162,810	33,180	289,926
1980	296,903	255,192	49,187	360,517
1985	382,022	336,403	52,691	355,113
1990	465,560	457,926	64,605	545,809
1993	487,249	489,137	63,951	537,111

Sources: Data before 1970 are from Civil Aeronautics Board, *Handbook of Airline Statistics, 1973 Edition* (March 1974). Data from 1970 on are from Air Transport Association, *Air Transport: The Annual Report of the U.S. Scheduled Airline Industry* (various years).
a. Figure is for 1927, the earliest available.

Industry Structure

Deregulation dramatically changed the structure of the airline industry. As some proponents had expected, competition exploded in the late 1970s and early 1980s as People Express, Air Florida, and other new carriers challenged the established airlines. But during the later 1980s the industry underwent severe consolidation. With the exception of Southwest, the new interstate entrants disappeared.

Of the carriers with annual revenues greater than $1 billion (the major carriers) that have remained in the industry, American is the leader in revenue, but United leads in passenger miles and Delta in enplanements (table 2-2). These three measures create an ambiguous ranking because airlines differ in the types of routes they fly, which is indicated by their average lengths of haul (that is, the average passenger trip distance, which is passenger miles divided by enplanements). United's long average length of haul (with its correspondingly low fare per mile) makes it a runner-up in revenue although it leads in passenger miles. Southwest's highly publicized regional service stands out clearly; its length of haul is

conclusions about deregulation are affected when we use an earlier starting date. One database that we use extensively (Department of Transportation Data Bank 1A) includes fare data only since October 1978.

Table 2-2.   *Enplanements, Passenger Miles, Average Length of Haul, and Revenue, by Major Carrier, 1993*

Carrier	Enplanements (thousands)	Passenger miles (millions)	Average length of haul (miles)	Revenue (millions of 1993 dollars)
American	82,536	97,062	1,176	14,737
United	69,672	100,991	1,450	14,354
Delta	84,813	82,863	977	12,376
Northwest	44,098	58,033	1,316	8,448
USAir	53,679	35,220	656	6,623
Continental	37,280	39,859	1,069	5,086
TWA	18,938	22,664	1,197	3,094
Southwest	37,517	16,716	446	2,067
America West	14,700	11,188	761	1,332

Source: Air Transport Association, *Air Transport, 1994* (Washington, 1994), p. 5.

the shortest of any major carrier. The size of the major carriers also varies considerably: American's revenue is more than eleven times greater than America West's.

To casual observers, deregulation seemed merely to have led to fewer airlines. But according to transportation officials, more operated at the end of 1993 (seventy-six) than at the end of 1978 (forty-three). A simple count, however, is a misleading indicator of the extent of competition because it assigns equal importance to a small carrier and a giant. One way to overcome this false comparison is to calculate the number of effective competitors, which is the inverse of the Herfindahl index.[2] Based on this index, figure 2-1 shows that the number of effective competitors at the national level increased from fewer than nine in the fourth quarter of 1978 to a peak of more than twelve in 1985. Then a wave of

2. Interpreting an inverted Herfindahl index as a "numbers-equivalent" was suggested by M. A. Adelman, "Comment on the 'H' Concentration Measure as a Numbers-Equivalent," *Review of Economics and Statistics*, vol. 51 (February 1969), pp. 99–101. The index approaches zero in the competitive case with a large number of small firms, and equals one in the monopoly case, so its inverse approaches infinity in the competitive case and equals one for monopoly. The inverse may be thought of as giving the number of equal-sized competitors that would provide a degree of competition equivalent to that actually observed in the market-share data. The index captures inequality in market shares by summing the square of each airline's market share. For example, if two airlines each have a 50 percent market share, the Herfindahl index is $0.50^2 + 0.50^2 = 1/2$. Inverting this gives 2 (effective competitors). Similarly, the index for three equal-sized airlines is $3 \times 0.33^2 = 1/3$, so inversion gives three effective competitors. But if there were three competitors, with the largest serving 2/3 of the market and the other two each serving 1/6 of the market, the Herfindahl index would be 1/2, which also translates into two effective competitors. Thus *effective competitors* has a more intuitive interpretation than the Herfindahl index.

Figure 2-1. *Airline Industry Effective Competitors, National Level,*
1978–93

Number of effective competitors

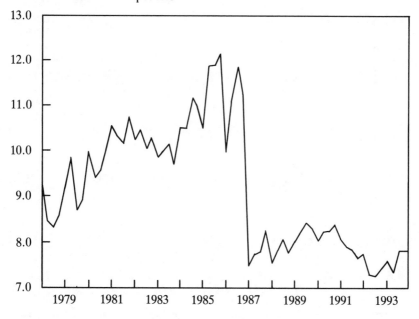

Sources: Authors' calculations using Department of Transportation Data Bank 1A, a 10 percent sample of airline tickets. The number of effective competitors at the national level is calculated based on each carrier's share of domestic passenger miles.

fourteen mergers between June 1985 and October 1987 reduced the number to slightly fewer than had existed before deregulation.

But if fewer effective competitors exist at the national level, deregulation has not necessarily decreased airline competition: for it is at the *route* level that airlines compete head to head. For example, four effective competitors at the national level can operate in two very different ways: with each having a monopoly share on one-quarter of the routes or with each having a one-quarter share on all routes. Although the number of airlines is the same either way, the second situation is obviously more competitive because more airlines serve each route. Thus fewer effective competitors at the national level does not necessarily mean that the industry is less competitive.

To measure competition at the route level, we calculated the number of effective competitors on each route; we then averaged over all routes, weighting both by passengers and by passenger miles (figure 2-2). The

Figure 2-2.   *Airline Industry Effective Competitors, Route Level, 1978–93*

Number of effective competitors

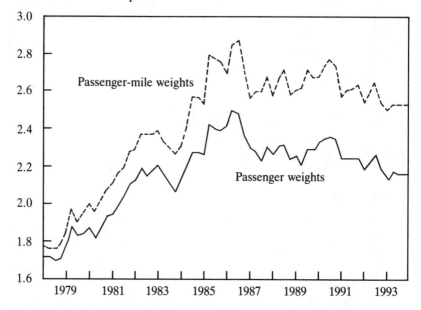

Sources: Authors' calculations using Department of Transportation Data Bank 1A. Each airline's share of passengers on each domestic route was calculated from a subsample of one-way tickets with two or fewer segments and round-trip tickets with two or fewer segments on the outbound and return legs. These route-level measures were aggregated across routes based on the percentage of sampled passengers and passenger miles on each route.

two measures diverge because more carriers have entered long-haul routes, and long-haul routes have a greater importance when passenger-mile weights are used than when passenger weights are. But the trend is clear with either measure. Competition increased steadily until mid-1986, decreased because of mergers, then reversed course in mid-1989 and increased through the third quarter of 1990. The decline during the fourth quarter of 1990 and the first quarter of 1991 reflects the liquidation of Eastern Airlines and economic recession. Even so, at the route level airlines are clearly more competitive than they were under regulation.[3]

3. As an alternative measure to the number of effective competitors, we calculated from the Department of Transportation's Data Bank 1A ticket sample the percentage of passengers on carriers with different market shares. This calculation led to findings consistent with those obtained by using the number of effective competitors. In particular, the percentage of passengers flying on carriers with less than a 20 percent route market share more than doubled, from 7.2 percent to 15.2 percent, between 1978 and 1993. During that

Figure 2-3. *Domestic Airline Average Fare per Passenger Mile (Yield),*
1970–93

1993 constant dollars

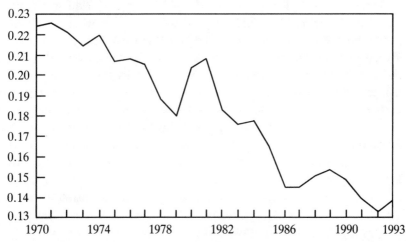

Sources: Domestic yield is from authors' calculations using Air Transport Association, *Air Transport:*
The Annual Report of the U.S. Scheduled Airline Industry, various issues. Real yield was calculated by
adjusting nominal yield using the consumer price index.

But as the differences between the passenger-weighted and passenger-mile-weighted figures suggest, competition has not been uniform on short and long routes. In particular, the number of effective competitors on routes shorter than 500 miles fell by 2 percent between 1978 and 1993, while the number on routes longer than 2,000 miles increased by 70 percent. Under deregulation, then, there are fewer effective competitors nationally, but carriers compete at the route level more often. What has been the effect on fares, service quality, profitability, and safety?

Fares

Fares are the focus of any discussion of the airline industry. As with competition, the measure used is important. The standard measure of fares, *yield*, is the average fare per mile for trips by paying customers. As figure 2-3 shows, yield adjusted for inflation had been falling even before deregulation. After more than a decade and a half of deregulation,

---

same period the percentage of passengers flying on carriers with route monopolies (100 percent route market share) fell from 10.2 percent to 5.6 percent.

real yield in 1993 was two-thirds of its value in 1976. Can this decrease be attributed to deregulation or, because of underlying factors such as technological change, would it have occurred with or without regulation?

These questions can be analyzed empirically, but to do so we must compare the actual (nominal) deregulated yield with what fares *would have been* had they remained regulated by the Civil Aeronautics Board. We estimated these regulated fares by updating the fare formula (called the standard industry fare level, or SIFL) used by the CAB during the last few years of regulation. Although there is no way of knowing for certain what regulated fares would be today, there is no evidence to suggest that before deregulation the CAB was making or would have made fundamental changes in its fare structure. Indeed, the board believed that it was taking a rational cost-based approach to regulating fares.

The SIFL is still calculated by the Department of Transportation, not for regulatory purposes but for use by the Internal Revenue Service in valuing free trips on corporate aircraft. Every six months the department calculates a SIFL cost adjustment factor based on observed changes in cost per available seat mile. But to use these factors to update the SIFL would have been misleading for our purposes. We needed to know what the cost per available seat mile (and the SIFL) would have been if airlines were still regulated. If deregulation has kept costs lower than what they would have been, the unadjusted SIFL would be too low. Using data developed by Douglas W. Caves and his colleagues, we estimated that between 1976 and 1983 (when their study ended) deregulation increased passenger-mile productivity growth 1.3 to 1.6 percent a year.[4] We started with the midpoint of this range. But some of this productivity increase was due to greater load factors, which had to be excluded from the calculation because SIFL adjustments are based on seat-mile costs, not passenger-mile costs. Adjusting for changes in load factor reduced the measured productivity change by 0.25 percentage point a year, resulting in a midpoint productivity change of 1.2 percent a year. We thus increased the observed SIFL by 1.2 percent a year from 1976 to 1983. By 1983 this resulted in an 8.7 percent increase. Arguably, productivity growth continued to increase after 1983 because of deregulation, although at a reduced rate, so the use of a midpoint figure only through 1983 should

4. Douglas W. Caves and others, "An Assessment of the Efficiency Effects of U.S. Airline Deregulation via an International Comparison," in Elizabeth E. Bailey, ed., *Public Regulation: New Perspectives on Institutions and Policies* (MIT Press, 1987), pp. 285–320.

err on the side of conservatism; that is, in all likelihood the extent that deregulation has lowered fares is understated. We were also being conservative by assuming in this calculation that factor prices were unchanged by deregulation.[5]

The line for actual yield in figure 2-4 was calculated based on ticket prices in a subsample of Department of Transportation Data Bank 1A.[6] The line for regulated yield was calculated by pricing all the tickets in the actual yield calculation using an estimated fare implied by the adjusted SIFL. As the figure shows, actual yields have been consistently lower than regulated yields would have been, although the gap has varied. The largest percentage differences occurred during the 1981–82 and 1990–91 recessions, when rising fuel prices increased airline costs and thus would also have increased regulated fares. But during these recessions *deregulated* carriers lowered fares to attract what business was available. On average, deregulation has led to fares 22 percent lower than they would have been had regulation continued.[7] The annual saving to flyers has been about $12.4 billion in 1993 dollars.[8] During 1993, fares

5. According to previous research, deregulation, to the extent it had any impact, lowered the cost of labor. See, for example, David Card, "Deregulation and Labor Earnings in the Airline Industry," Princeton University, Princeton Industrial Relations Section working paper 247, January 1989.

6. The subsample was all domestic round-trip tickets with two or fewer segments on each of the outbound and return legs. Tickets with fares that were unreasonably high were excluded. Tickets with fares that seemed too low reflected coding errors and legitimate frequent flier awards. The percentage of tickets with low fares was stable (an average 1.7 percent of tickets and 2.5 percent of passenger miles) from the fourth quarter of 1978 to the fourth quarter of 1986, when it began to increase. We assumed that any subsequent increase in the percentage of low-fare tickets was due to frequent flier tickets. From the first quarter of 1987 to the fourth quarter of 1993 this averaged 4.0 percent of passengers and 5.5 percent of passenger miles. We then divided revenue earned on tickets with "good" fares by the sum of "good" passenger miles plus our estimate of frequent flier passenger miles to obtain actual yield.

7. It can be argued that this type of estimate becomes increasingly uncertain as time goes on, but this view is shaped by evidence based on the deregulated experience that reveals flaws in CAB regulation. That is, any belief that fare regulation would have caused less expense for travelers presumes that the regulatory authority would have learned from past errors and would have been able to avoid them when developing a new regulatory fare structure. There is not much evidence to support this view. Moreover, we were interested in calculating the difference between regulated and deregulated fares over time as opposed to calculating the difference between regulated and deregulated fares assuming that regulated fares are partly based on previous experience with deregulated fares.

8. This figure represents how much more money travelers would have paid if fares had remained regulated for trips they actually took under deregulated fares. The figure overstates travelers' gain because, on average, fares fell, generating more trips than would have

Figure 2-4. *Airline Industry Average Fare per Passenger Mile (Yield), Actual under Deregulation and Projected under Regulation, 1978–93*

Current dollars

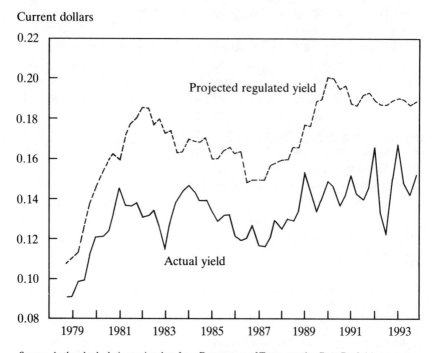

Source: Authors' calculations using data from Department of Transportation Data Bank 1A; see text.

were 19 percent lower than they would have been under regulation. Real fares (figure 2-3) have declined about 33 percent since 1976 (that is, before any significant regulatory reforms by the CAB). Thus deregulation has accounted for 58 percent (19/33) of the observed decrease in real air fares.[9]

Although CAB fare regulation led to higher fares, is it possible that a more enlightened, less harmful type of regulation could be put into

occurred under higher regulated fares. The figure was obtained by multiplying, for each quarter from the fourth quarter of 1978 to the fourth quarter of 1993, real domestic passenger revenue by the percentage that adjusted SIFL fares exceed actual (deregulated) fares and taking the annual average of the result.

9. Using data covering a much shorter time than is covered here, and without using methodologies that relied on adjusting the SIFL, we also found in 1986 that deregulation had lowered fares. See Steven Morrison and Clifford Winston, *The Economic Effects of Airline Deregulation* (Brookings, 1986). We obtained this result by comparing actual regulated fares in 1977 with predictions based on actual 1983 deregulated fares of what deregulated fares would have been during this period.

Table 2-3.   *U.S., North American, and World Airline Industry Average Fares per Passenger Mile (Yield), 1969, 1980, 1990, 1991*[a]

Year	Distances (miles)	U.S. or North American yield (dollars)	World yield (dollars)	Percentage difference
1969	All	0.40 (U.S. only)	0.42	−4.8
1980	All	0.76 (U.S. only)	0.88	−13.6
1990	All	0.87 (U.S. only)	1.13	−23.0
1991	150	0.35	0.37	−5.4
	300	0.25	0.29	−13.8
	600	0.18	0.23	−21.7
	1,200	0.13	0.19	−31.6
	2,400	0.09	0.15	−40.0

Source: Authors' calculations based on unpublished data from the International Civil Aviation Organization.

a. Yields for 1991 are in dollars per revenue passenger mile; yields for other years are in dollars per ton-kilometers performed. World yield for 1991 includes the North American yield; world yield for other years does not include U.S. yield.

practice? The 1975–78 experience suggests that enlightened regulation is possible but that regulatory performance depends very much on the personalities involved, particularly that of the CAB chairman. Furthermore, for an alternative regulatory fare structure to improve very much on the CAB's effort, it would still have to adjust rapidly and accurately to carriers' costs and the demand on their capacity. It is unlikely that a regulatory body could design and implement a fare structure with that feature.

Low U.S. airfares have not escaped the notice of other countries. Table 2-3 compares 1991 yields at various distances in North America with the world average for the same distances. The differential is what one would expect when comparing regulated and deregulated fares and provides additional evidence that U.S. fares would have been higher if left regulated. The table also shows that international fare differences have grown significantly since U.S. deregulation in 1978.[10] The widening gap has already prompted Japan, Canada, and Australia to deregulate their fares. Countries in the European Union plan to deregulate theirs in 1997.

10. Fare differences between countries could reflect differences in average trip distance. The significant finding here, however, is the trend in the percentage difference.

Figure 2-5. *Distribution of Fares Travelers Paid Relative to Their Route's Average Fare, Fourth Quarter 1978, 1985, 1993*

Percent of travelers

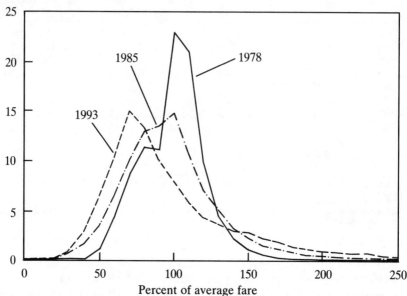

Percent of average fare

Source: Authors' calculations based on a subsample of Department of Transportation Data Bank 1A, a 10 percent sample of airline tickets. Subsample was all domestic round-trip tickets with two or fewer segments outbound and two or fewer segments return. To correct for possible coding errors in the data airlines submitted, tickets with fares that seemed unreasonably high or low were excluded. Thus frequent flier tickets were excluded.

Although deregulation has lowered average U.S. domestic fares, it has also led to the proliferation of fare categories, ranging from relatively expensive unrestricted coach seats to deeply discounted seats with a host of restrictions, on every carrier and for every route. To show this proliferation, figure 2-5 plots what percentage of travelers paid what percentage of the average fare on the route they traveled.[11] A glance confirms what travelers have believed for some time: the variability of fares has increased. Using the data to construct the figure, we found that in the fourth quarter of 1978, for instance, 37 percent of passengers paid fares that were less than or equal to the average fare, while only 2 percent paid more than 1.5 times the average. By the end of 1993, some 59 percent

11. To obtain a distribution for a given quarter, the variation on each route was weighted by the number of passengers traveling on that route.

were paying fares less than or equal to the average, and 13 percent were paying more than 1.5 times the average.

Some of the variation reflects cost-based price differences, such as those between higher peak and lower off-peak fares. Cost differences also arise because business travelers place a much higher value than pleasure travelers on the convenience of booking a seat at the last minute. Airlines therefore carry a larger inventory of seats for business travelers relative to their expected demand than they do for pleasure travelers. The cost of these extra seats is reflected in the higher unrestricted fares business travelers pay. Some additional price variation is due to the proliferation of so-called niche carriers such as Reno Air, which stimulates a greater range of fare offerings by all carriers. Finally, the wider variation reflects carriers' increased efforts to align their fares more closely with passengers' willingness to pay for air travel. (This practice, known as price discrimination, is discussed in chapter 4.) The benefit for travelers and carriers is that carriers can use discount prices to fill seats that would otherwise be vacant.

The results in figure 2-5, in combination with the increase in competition at the route level shown in figure 2-2, suggest that the increase in airline competition has led to a wider dispersion of fares. Is this interpretation correct? Intuition suggests otherwise; perfect competition, for example, should cause prices to converge—the law of one price. To resolve this matter empirically, we constructed measures of a carrier's spread of fares on a route, then regressed this variable on characteristics of the route and the level of competition on it, including the number of effective competitors.[12] We did this separately for each quarter from the

---

12. The basic unit of observation was the spread of a carrier's fares on a route. The data set was from the ten largest carriers nationwide in 1993 for the 1,000 most heavily traveled domestic routes. Separate regressions were run for each quarter from the fourth quarter of 1978 to the fourth quarter of 1993. Four measures of the spread of fares were used: the real standard deviation of fares, the standard deviation divided by the mean (the coefficient of variation), the eightieth percentile of real fares minus the twentieth percentile of real fares, and that percentile difference divided by the fiftieth percentile fare. The results did not change regardless of which spread measure we used. We also considered alternative assumptions regarding the minimum number of passengers an airline had to carry to qualify as serving a route during a particular quarter. Our base case was 600 sampled passengers a quarter (Department of Transportation Data Bank 1A is a 10 percent sample of airline tickets), which is equivalent to one flight a day. The findings were not particularly sensitive to alternative assumptions. Finally, the independent variables were route distance, carrier dummy variables to capture airline-specific effects, dummy variables for each airport on the route that is subject to capacity controls that effectively limit entry

Figure 2-6.   *Effect of an Additional Competitor on the Spread of
Airline Fares on a Route, Fourth Quarter 1978 to Fourth Quarter 1993*

Current dollars

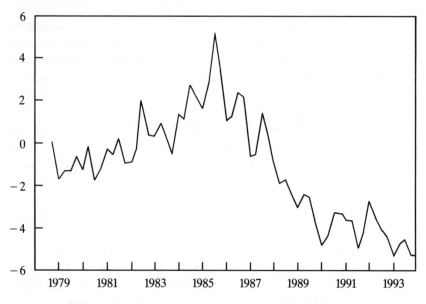

Source: Authors' calculations. Each entry is the effect of an additional effective competitor on the real standard deviation of each carrier's fares on each of its domestic routes (that is, the coefficient of the number of effective competitors from a regression for a given quarter). See text for additional details.

fourth quarter of 1978 to the fourth quarter of 1993, and for several definitions of spread. With spread defined as the real standard deviation, the effect of airline competition on the spread of fares (the estimated coefficient of the effective competition variable in the fare regressions) is shown in figure 2-6.[13] Increased competition widened the spread of fares only after deregulation had been under way for a few years, perhaps because of the introduction of discount fares by People Express and other new entrants. That is, the established carriers lowered some of their fares to match those of the new entrants, but kept others unchanged.

(there are four of these slot-controlled airports), the number of effective competitors on the route, and the minimum number of effective competitors at the origin and destination airports.

   13. The pattern of results was unchanged when a 95 percent confidence interval of the coefficients is plotted instead of the point estimates.

Competition increased the spread of fares until the mid-1980s merger wave.[14] But since 1988, with relative stability in the level of national and route competition, the fares of carriers on routes with greater competition have less spread. Based on the data in the figure, during 1993 an additional competitor on a route decreased the spread 8 to 9 percent. Thus although the spread of fares for all carriers at the route level has grown since deregulation (see figure 2-5), after the late 1980s, increasing route competition reduced the spread of an individual carrier's fares.

With deregulation, another CAB regulatory practice, setting long-haul fares higher than cost to subsidize short-haul fares that were set below cost, also ended. Now that competitive forces and not a regulatory formula determine prices, real airfares have increased for distances of less than 800 miles and decreased for greater distances (figure 2-7).[15]

All these fare differences understandably obscure the finding that deregulation has substantially lowered average fares. Although 70 percent of passengers accounting for 78 percent of revenue passenger miles in the fourth quarter of 1993 paid fares less than or equal to what they would have had regulation continued (figure 2-8), not all travelers have benefited. Because of all the fare differences, 14 percent of passengers accounting for 10 percent of passenger miles are paying fares that are two or more times higher than they would have been had regulation continued. This new order is undoubtedly partly responsible for instances of public dissatisfaction with deregulation.

Service Quality

Fare increases or decreases are not the only matters to affect passenger welfare, of course. There is also the question of how deregulation has affected service. Service is something of an amorphous concept: it can cover everything from the quality of food provided by carriers to the

14. Severin Borenstein and Nancy L. Rose, "Competition and Price Dispersion in the U.S. Airline Industry," *Journal of Political Economy*, vol. 102 (August 1994), pp. 653–83, also found a positive relationship between route-level competition and the spread of fares during the second quarter of 1986.

15. Some low-density short routes are served by carriers receiving a subsidy under the essential air service provision of the Airline Deregulation Act. The subsidy was designed to ensure that no community that received air service by a CAB-regulated carrier would lose air service as a result of deregulation. Service to that community would be subsidized if no carrier was willing to offer unsubsidized service. Without the subsidy, short-haul fares would have risen somewhat more.

Figure 2-7. *Change in Domestic Air Fares, by Route Distance,*
Fourth Quarter 1978 to Fourth Quarter 1993

Percent change

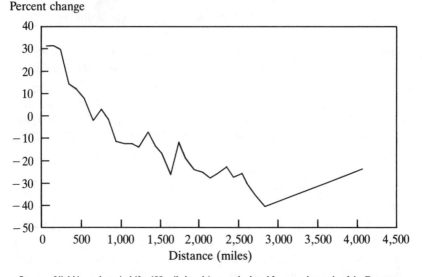

Distance (miles)

Sources: Yield in each period (for 100-mile bands) was calculated from a subsample of the Department of Transportation's 10 percent sample of airline tickets (Data Bank 1A). This subsample was all domestic round-trip tickets with two or fewer segments outbound and two or fewer segments return. To correct for possible coding errors in the data airlines submitted, a fare screen was used to screen out tickets with fares that seemed unreasonably high or low. Fares were adjusted for inflation using the consumer price index.

cheerfulness of flight attendants, from ease of check-in to the care taken in baggage handling, from the frequency of flights to how many direct flights are available to whether passengers need to switch airlines to reach their destination. Not all of these services are possible to quantify. But several key dimensions, including the frequency of service, how many passengers change flights, the length of travel time, and the level of restrictions on tickets, can be analyzed with some rigor.

By eliminating the old restrictions on which carriers could fly where, deregulation gave airlines increased freedom and flexibility to restructure their networks into hub-and-spoke systems that feed travelers from all directions into a major airport (hub) from which they take connecting flights to their destinations. The hub-and-spoke system has been adopted by nearly all carriers. American has established major hubs at Dallas–Fort Worth and Chicago, United at Denver and Chicago, Delta at Atlanta and Dallas–Fort Worth. Among smaller carriers, Southwest has hubs at Phoenix and Dallas Love Field and Reno Air at Reno. The system

Figure 2-8.   *Distribution of Domestic Air Fares Relative to Projected Regulated Fares, Fourth Quarter 1993*

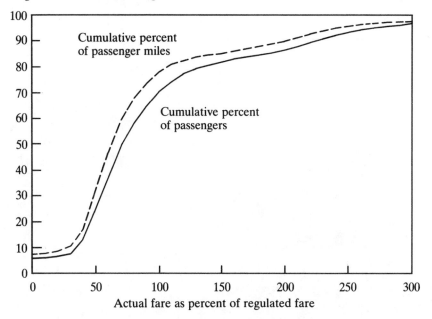

Actual fare as percent of regulated fare

Data Source and Variable Construction: Fares actually paid in 1993:4 are from a subsample of the Department of Transportation's 10 percent sample of airline tickets (Data Bank 1A). This subsample was all domestic round-trip tickets with two or fewer segments outbound and two or fewer segments return. To correct for possible coding errors in the data the airlines submitted, a fare screen was used to eliminate tickets with fares that seemed unreasonably high. Tickets with low fares were not removed in order not to remove valid frequent flier tickets. However, the percentage of zero-fare tickets was reduced by 1.7 percent of total tickets (2.5 percent of total passenger miles) to correct for coding errors. (See footnote 6 in this chapter for the origin of these correction factors.) For each ticket in the subsample, the fare actually paid was compared with an estimate of the regulated fare that would have been charged if fares were based on our adjusted standard industry fare level (SIFL) fare formula.

gives passengers from spokes and from the hub more frequent service than would be possible with single-plane service. The resulting benefits from the increased frequency over what was offered during regulation have been estimated at $10.3 billion a year in 1993 dollars.[16]

A familiar complaint about the hub-and-spoke system is that passengers are not flown by the shortest route to their destinations, that instead

16. This figure is from Morrison and Winston, *Economic Effects of Airline Deregulation*, p. 31—a gain per traveler from increased frequency of $8.00 times 539.3 million intercity trips converted to 1993 dollars. It reflects the value of increased frequency through 1983. We are not aware of more recent estimates. This finding was somewhat surprising.

Figure 2-9. *Share of All Passengers on Domestic Flights Who Needed to Make Connecting Flights, 1978–93*

Percent

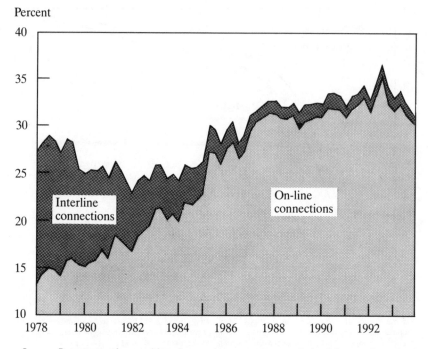

Sources: Percentage and composition of connecting passengers was calculated from a subsample of domestic trips in the Department of Transportation's 10 percent sample of airline tickets (Data Bank 1A). This subsample consisted of one-way tickets with two or fewer segments and round-trip tickets with two or fewer segments on the outbound and return legs.

they must take circuitous routings that require changing planes. But changing planes has not been much more frequent than it was before deregulation: 28 percent of passengers had to change in 1978 and about 32 percent in 1993 (figure 2-9). What has changed remarkably is the nature of the connections. In 1978 about half of passengers changing planes—14 percent of all passengers—also changed airlines. But with the freedom to enter new markets that was afforded by deregulation, airlines have been able to rationalize their route systems so that today only 1 percent of passengers must change airlines, an improvement in service

The traditional view of regulation was that because carriers were prevented from competing through fares they competed, in particular, through flight frequency. See, for example, George W. Douglas and James C. Miller III, *Economic Regulation of Domestic Air Transport: Theory and Policy* (Brookings, 1974).

because travelers prefer on-line to interline connections.[17] And despite the occasional apparent circuity of routing required by the hub-and-spoke system, excess air mileage has increased only about 1 percentage point (figure 2-10).[18] Thus we found that the net effect on travelers' welfare of fewer interline connections combined with more connections overall would seem to be beneficial, if slight (see the appendix to this chapter).

The benefits from hub-and-spoke systems have been partly offset by increased travel time, both on the ground and in the air (figure 2-11). The ground time has increased by about five minutes regardless of distance. (Because the data are for flight segments, time spent connecting between flights is not reflected.) This increase probably stems from greater airport and airway congestion in the wake of deregulation. The strike by air traffic controllers and the subsequent dismissal of trained personnel in 1981, events independent of deregulation, may also have contributed to congestion.[19]

The difference in travel time increases with distance, which is consistent with slower cruise speeds that are themselves perhaps the result of pilots' flying more slowly to conserve fuel and of the slower cruising speed of more recently developed aircraft. Because both influences are arguably independent of deregulation, this increase should not be entirely attributed to it. Nonetheless, if deregulation were responsible for the entire additional travel time, we estimate the cost to travelers at

17. Dennis W. Carlton, William M. Landes, and Richard A. Posner, "Benefits and Costs of Airline Mergers: A Case Study," *Bell Journal of Economics*, vol. 11 (Spring 1980), p. 73, estimate that travelers would be willing to pay between $13.10 and $17.75 (in 1977 dollars) more for a flight with an on-line connection than one with an interline connection. Using the midpoint of this range and converting it to 1993 dollars yields nearly $37 a traveler. The benefits from on-line connections include a shorter walk in the terminal to catch the connecting flight, greater coordination with the originating flight (for example, if it is delayed), and less chance of lost luggage.

18. Excess air mileage was calculated by comparing the miles actually flown by all passengers in our subsample of Data Bank 1A with the great circle distance (the shortest distance) from their origin to their destination. The matter of circuity also affects the debate about fares. The conventional approach to calculating yield has been to divide revenue by passenger miles actually traveled, not the (shorter) great circle distance from origin to destination. To the extent that circuity has increased, yields will be artificially low, reflecting the increased miles required to make a given trip. However, because the change in circuity from 1978–93 was only one percent, the error in fare comparisons over the same period was small—about 1 percent.

19. As discussed more fully in the final chapter, the negative effects of increased airport and airway congestion could be reduced by congestion-based takeoff and landing fees at airports as well as by expedited introduction of new technologies and operating procedures.

Figure 2-10.   *Excess of Actual Distance Flown over Shortest Possible Distance to Destination, Domestic Trips, 1978–93*

Percent excess miles

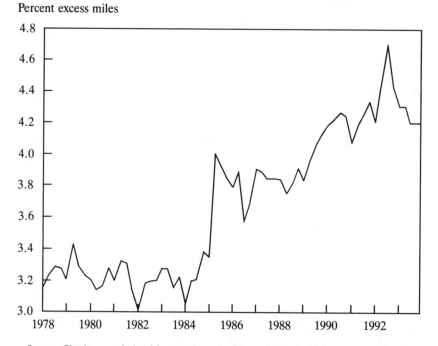

Sources: Circuity was calculated from a subsample of domestic trips in the Department of Transportation's 10 percent sample of airline tickets (Data Bank 1A). This subsample was all one-way tickets with two or fewer segments and round-trip tickets with two or fewer segments on the outbound and return legs. For all trips, the actual distance flown from origin to destination was compared with the shortest (that is, the great circle) distance from origin to destination. The circuity figures above involve the percentage of passengers connecting times the circuity of connections. Percentage of passengers connecting has increased from about 28 percent in 1978 to about 32 percent in 1993. During the same time the circuity of connections increased from about 11 percent to 13 percent.

$2.8 billion in 1993 dollars.[20] The increase in flight time since deregulation, and its cost to travelers, does appear to have stabilized (figure 2-12). After expanding steadily since 1983, the additional flight time peaked in 1990 at about 9 minutes and has remained close to that level even though passenger enplanements have continued to expand.

20. From the data for figure 2-11, we derived a passenger-weighted average of 9.0 minutes' increase in total flight time for each flight segment. Multiplying the average number of passenger segments (enplanements) from 1978–93 by 9.0 minutes and using the value of travel time, updated to 1993 dollars, in Steven A. Morrison and Clifford Winston, "Enhancing the Performance of the Deregulated Air Transportation System," *Brookings Papers*

Figure 2-11.   *Change in Components of Total Flight Time, Domestic Flights, by Flight Distance, 1978–93*

Minutes

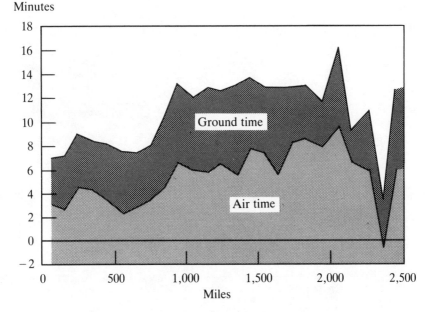

Sources: Calculated from the domestic flight data in the Department of Transportation Service Segment Data Base, a complete census of airline flight segments that gives monthly totals for actual (not scheduled) air and ground time at the route level. Because the data are for flight segments, time spent connecting between flights is not reflected. Variability for distances greater than 2,000 miles is because there are fewer routes over which to average.

Deregulation has reduced service convenience in some ways. On average it has filled more planes and made it harder for travelers to get a seat on the flight of their choice (figure 2-13). The increase in the percentage of seats filled, called the industry load factor, is likely to cost travelers $0.6 billion annually in 1993 dollars.[21] But the higher load factor

on *Economic Activity: Microeconomics* (1989), p. 66 (the original estimate was $34.04 an hour in 1983 dollars), yields the figure in the text.

21. This estimate used the schedule delay formula developed by Douglas and Miller, *Economic Regulation of Domestic Air Transport*. We assumed that without deregulation the load factor would have remained at its 1977 value of 55.9 percent (Morrison and Winston, *Economic Effects of Airline Deregulation*, p. 35). This ignores any possible long-term growth in load factors that may have occurred during regulation, thus inflating our cost estimate. For each year from 1978 to 1993 we calculated the difference between schedule delay using the 1977 figure and the actual figure for that year (assuming routes had 1,000 passengers a day and an aircraft with 150 seats). Valuing schedule delay at the rate used by Morrison and Winston, *Economic Effects of Airline Deregulation*, and mul-

Figure 2-12.   *Change in Components of Total Flight Time,*
Domestic Flights, 1978–93

Minutes

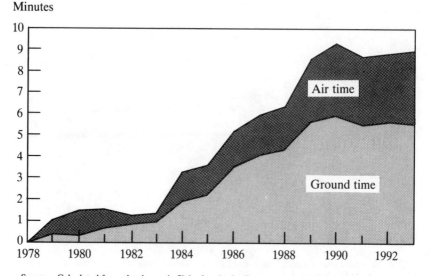

Sources: Calculated from the domestic flight data in the Department of Transportation Service Segment Data Base, a complete census of airline flight segments that gives monthly totals for actual (not scheduled) air and ground time at the route level. Only those routes that were served in all years from 1978 to 1993 are included in the calculation. Flight times are aggregated across routes using the number of passengers in 1978 as weights. Because the data are for flight segments time spent connecting between flights is not reflected.

has helped to hold average costs and fares down during deregulation. Between 1978 and 1993 load factors fell for flights shorter than 1,000 miles and rose for longer flights (figure 2-14)—an expected effect given the CAB's fare policies, which elevated long-haul fares in order to subsidize short-haul fares, and the postderegulation fare changes that increased fares on the shorter flights (see figure 2-7).[22] The inverse relationship between fare and load factor changes indicates that some of the benefits from lower long distance fares have been compromised by the greater

tiplying by the average number of enplanements from 1978 to 1993 yielded the figure in the text. To be sure, using an average load factor does not account for the variation in load factors across city pairs. However, because of the nonlinear relation between load factors and schedule delay, load factors probably need to be consistently in the 65–70 percent range, which is typically greater than current levels, to generate large welfare losses from the difficulty in obtaining a seat on a preferred flight.

22. The 1978 load factors reflect the effect of less stringent application of CAB fare policy leading up to deregulation. Douglas and Miller, *Economic Regulation of Domestic Air Transport,* found that load factors in 1969 actually decreased with distance because of CAB fare policies.

Figure 2-13.   *Share of Airline Seats Filled by Paying Passengers*
(Load Factor), 1970–93

Percent

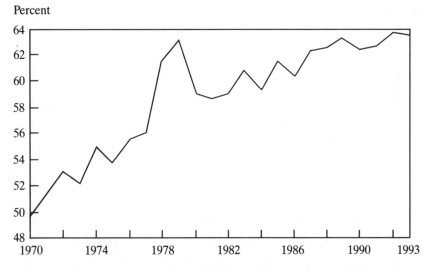

Source: Air Transport Association, *Air Transport: The Annual Report of the U.S. Scheduled Airline Industry* (various years). Load factor is the percentage of seats filled with paying passengers. It is calculated by dividing revenue-passenger miles by available seat miles (for both international and domestic service).

difficulty of obtaining a seat on a desired flight. And some of the increases in short-distance fares have been counterbalanced by a better chance of getting a seat on a desired flight. But given an annual cost of only $0.6 billion, the effect on consumers of this deterioration in service quality has been slight.

Service convenience has also been compromised by travel restrictions—advance purchase requirements, cancellation penalties, a mandatory Saturday night stay, and so on—attached to discount fares. Minimum stay and Saturday night stay requirements have perhaps caused more inconvenience than increased load factors because they may have forced customers to think about staying more days to get the lower fare rather than consider traveling during off-peak hours or making other compromises.

Deregulation has, then, led to some significant improvements in service quality, especially more frequent flights and less necessity for changing airlines to make connections. These benefits must be balanced against reductions in service quality attributable to more crowded flights, slightly longer flight times because of more congestion, a few more connections,

Figure 2-14. *Share of Airline Seats Filled by Paying Passengers,
by Distance, Domestic Flights, 1978, 1993*

Percent

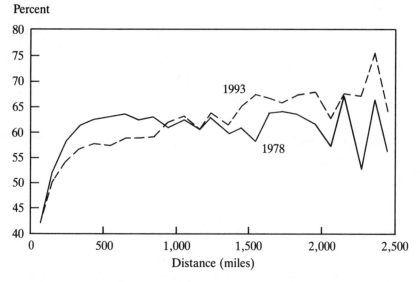

Source: Authors' calculations based on data in the Department of Transportation Service Segment
Data Base, a complete census of airline flights.

and fare restrictions, whose costs are quantified in chapter 4. We will
assess these costs and benefits, along with the benefits from lower fares,
after evaluating whether certain carrier practices could erode the benefits
from deregulation.

Profits

One thing is certain. The industry has not been earning excessive
profits.[23] Although operating profits among individual carriers have always varied (table 2-4), from 1990 to 1993 nearly all carriers experienced

23. There are many ways to measure profit. Economists' preferred approach is to
estimate a return to capital. Other approaches are operating (gross) profit margin, net
profit margin, return to equity, and so on. Return to capital, the best definition concep-
tually, suffers from the difficulty of obtaining the data, in particular, market values, needed
to measure it. Although less appropriate for some purposes, the other measures are easier
to calculate. For example, the operating profit margin is simply the difference between
revenue and cost, where cost does not include income taxes or interest on long-term debt,
expressed as a percentage of revenue. In this book we frequently focus on the operating
profit margin because it could be constructed from readily available data and, because it
excludes interest on long-term debt, was invariant to a firm's capital structure.

Table 2-4. Operating Profit Margins, Selected Airlines, 1970–93
Percent

Year	American	Continental	Delta	Eastern	America West	Northwest	Pan American	TWA	United	USAir	Southwest
1970	-1.33	6.98	12.20	4.42	. . .	13.49	-3.61	-7.32	-1.40	6.12	n.a.
1971	2.30	9.16	8.97	3.40	. . .	4.30	-3.04	1.19	2.27	3.66	n.a.
1972	3.05	9.36	11.45	4.58	. . .	3.88	-1.12	5.29	4.40	6.59	n.a.
1973	-2.45	3.93	11.01	-1.55	. . .	8.84	-0.21	4.80	7.73	6.06	n.a.
1974	2.38	10.23	12.03	4.62	. . .	10.20	-6.21	-1.05	7.96	5.00	n.a.
1975	-1.59	6.57	4.96	0.39	. . .	6.13	-2.10	-4.53	-0.24	0.85	n.a.
1976	3.39	6.82	7.84	4.34	. . .	10.65	0.82	2.61	1.29	4.13	n.a.
1977	2.70	6.81	9.31	1.69	. . .	10.02	4.57	1.83	2.72	5.23	n.a.
1978	3.55	5.53	9.64	4.07	. . .	8.55	6.30	1.98	8.22	6.03	n.a.
1979	-0.06	-2.23	4.63	3.85	. . .	4.33	2.80	-1.52	-7.34	7.13	19.96
1980	-3.07	-6.27	4.97	0.05	. . .	-1.46	-3.56	-1.09	-1.55	9.40	22.92
1981	1.11	-5.55	2.37	-1.34	. . .	0.11	-10.53	0.11	-3.28	5.27	17.94
1982	-0.46	-5.06	-2.37	-0.50	. . .	-0.42	-10.74	-3.22	-1.49	6.23	11.84
1983	5.51	-13.29	-1.46	-2.54	-35.52	3.14	0.37	-1.96	2.88	9.00	15.29
1984	6.66	8.99	6.39	4.35	-7.01	3.93	-4.00	2.06	9.02	11.83	12.81
1985	8.64	8.98	4.88	4.60	7.73	2.88	-6.58	-1.65	-6.67	9.54	11.60
1986	6.69	6.98	5.00	1.44	1.20	4.16	-13.63	-2.38	-0.15	9.19	13.13
1987	6.64	0.68	7.13	1.30	-6.13	4.04	-5.46	5.93	1.92	12.73	5.91
1988	9.37	1.72	7.10	-5.39	2.32	3.50	-2.93	5.95	7.14	5.13	10.00
1989	7.34	3.16	7.82	-55.73	4.82	4.43	-8.83	0.54	4.74	-5.42	9.61
1990	0.62	-4.65	-2.69	-24.45	-2.39	-1.95	-12.48	-3.52	-0.50	-8.93	6.88
1991	0.14	-5.09	-2.65	. . .	-7.37	-0.80	-22.39	-9.52	-4.21	-3.34	4.72
1992	-0.57	-3.73	-7.09	. . .	-5.74	-3.88	. . .	-10.35	-3.90	-6.02	10.79
1993	3.82	-0.91	-2.22	. . .	9.09	3.92	. . .	-8.02	2.06	-1.94	13.60

Source: Authors' calculations based on Department of Transportation form 41. Data include both international and domestic operations of the airlines. Operating profit margin is the difference between revenue and cost expressed as a percentage of revenue, where cost does not include interest on long-term debt and income taxes. (Eastern ceased operating in early 1991. Pan American ceased operating in late 1991. America West began operating in 1983. Although operating, Southwest did not have to file form 41 until 1979.)
n.a. Not available.

heavy losses, for a total of several billion dollars. Some carriers went into bankruptcy, and Eastern, Pan American, and Midway Airlines were liquidated, prompting speculation that only a few carriers might survive the current shakeout.[24] But amidst all the bad news, Southwest Airlines, under the colorful and innovative leadership of Herbert Kelleher, developed into a highly profitable carrier, generating an average operating profit margin of nearly 9 percent between 1990 and 1993.[25] As we discuss later, although Southwest is the next-to-smallest major carrier, with revenues about one-seventh those of American Airlines, its low-cost operations offer an intriguing glimpse of the direction in which some parts of the industry appear to be headed.

Figure 2-15 shows the operating profit margin (for both domestic and international service) for U.S. scheduled airlines from 1970 to 1993. Given the amount of stockholders' equity outstanding and the carriers' long-term debt, earning a "normal" 12 percent pretax return on investment would require an operating margin of about 5 percent.[26] This rate has seldom been achieved either before or since deregulation. The industry's poor performance during regulation reflects another failing of regulatory policy, which was to have set fare levels that, at least in principle, would have enabled carriers to earn a normal rate of return. They did not, and deregulation has not remedied the situation. Indeed, the

---

24. A commonly cited estimate of the extent of losses during 1990–93 for both domestic and international service is $12.8 billion (after tax and interest payments), based on data in Air Transport Association, *Air Transport, 1994: The Annual Report of the U.S. Scheduled Airline Industry* (Washington, 1994), p. 3. This figure is potentially misleading because it includes losses due to changes in accounting practices (affecting all industries). Since 1992 the Financial Accounting Standards Board (through FASB 106) has required businesses to record retiree benefits and other liabilities that they always assumed but were not required to report. This change accounts for $2.2 billion of the losses reported earlier. In addition, the staggering losses of a few carriers (those that were in bankruptcy: Pan American, Eastern, TWA, and Continental), amounting to $5.6 billion, make the industry as a whole look sicker than it is. Finally, these losses exaggerate the true financial picture because the accounting charge for depreciation of airline assets (mostly airplanes) typically exceeds the true decline in the value of the assets. Notwithstanding these qualifications, by any measure the airlines did sustain considerable losses during the early 1990s.

25. Richard S. Teitelbaum, "Southwest Airlines: Where Service Flies Right," *Fortune*, August 24, 1992, p. 115, estimated that Southwest generated a 26.5 percent annualized return to investors from 1987 to 1992.

26. The 5 percent figure is the approximate operating profit margin that would be required from 1976 to 1993 to enable gross profits to be 12 percent of long-term debt and stockholders' equity.

Figure 2-15. *Scheduled Airline Operating Profit Margin for Domestic and International Services, 1970–93*

Percent

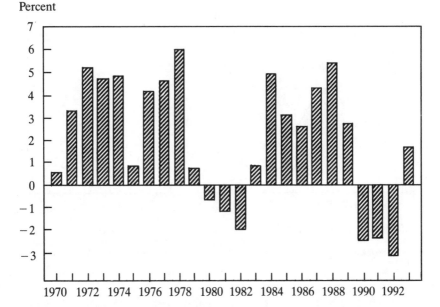

Source: Air Transport Association, *Air Transport: The Annual Report of the U.S. Scheduled Airline Industry* (various years). Operating profit margin is the percentage by which revenue exceeds cost, where cost does not include interest on long-term debt and income taxes and includes both domestic and international operations.

major concern today is whether the industry can be profitable at all for a protracted period.

Safety

When deregulation took effect in 1978, industry analysts feared that the new competitive conditions could affect airline safety in two ways.[27] Some speculated that unregulated competition would lead to lower prof-

27. For complete discussions of airline deregulation and airline safety see Clinton V. Oster, Jr., John S. Strong, and C. Kurt Zorn, *Why Airplanes Crash: Aviation Safety in a Changing World* (Oxford University Press, 1992); and Nancy L. Rose, "Fear of Flying? Economic Analyses of Airline Safety," *Journal of Economic Perspectives*, vol. 6 (Spring 1992), pp. 75–94.

Figure 2-16.   *Chance of Death per Million Airline Departures, 1975–93*

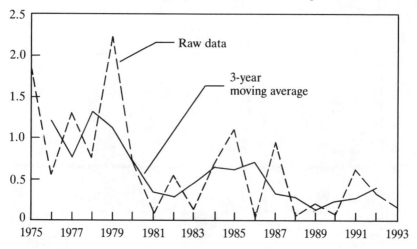

Source: Authors' calculations based on unpublished accident data from the National Transportation Safety Board for air carriers (part 121) and commuters (part 135). The probability of death is calculated by multiplying fatal accidents per departure by the percentage of passengers involved in fatal accidents who die.

its, prompting airlines to skimp on maintenance.[28] And there was also concern that as commuter airlines replaced larger airlines at small cities, safety records might deteriorate because of the higher accident rate of commuter carriers. But in the past two decades, as figure 2-16 shows, air travel safety for commuter and larger airlines combined has improved. Because the raw data are so volatile from year to year, the figure uses a moving average to smooth out the fluctuations and emphasize the underlying trend. Safety therefore should be the least controversial concern

28. Oster, Strong, and Zorn, *Why Airplanes Crash*, have noted that most researchers have found no relationship between lower profits and reduced safety. An exception is Nancy L. Rose, "Profitability and Product Quality: Economic Determinants of Airline Safety Performance," *Journal of Political Economy*, vol. 98 (October 1990), pp. 944–64, who found that lower profitability was associated with higher accident rates, particularly for smaller carriers. But, as Oster, Strong, and Zorn pointed out, the mechanism linking the two is unclear because, for example, there is little correlation between changes in profits and maintenance expenditures per available seat mile. D. Mark Kennet, "Did Deregulation Affect Aircraft Engine Maintenance? An Empirical Policy Analysis," *Rand Journal of Economics*, vol. 24 (Winter 1993), pp. 542–58, examined one aspect of maintenance and found that deregulated airlines have increased the time between major overhauls of jet engines. But he also found that this did not lead to any increase in the likelihood of an engine failure. Kennet suggests that airline maintenance was not optimized before 1978 but has been since.

about air transportation. Regardless of how it is measured, only one conclusion can be reached: the chance of dying in an airplane crash continues to diminish.

Implications

What does this empirical profile reveal about the current state of air transportation? And what does it bode for the future? Although the number of effective competitors at the national level has declined since deregulation, competition on routes has increased. As a result, the long-run decrease in real air fares has continued, a trend largely attributable to deregulation. The greater variation of fares, both within and across routes, reflects differences in cost and in travelers' willingness to pay for different services, a willingness that could not be revealed because of the regulatory fare structure. Travelers have experienced deterioration in the quality of some aspects of service—flight times are now slightly longer, for example—but other and perhaps more important elements, especially the greater frequency of flights, have improved. The key question, then, would seem to be can the fare and service benefits consumers have received from deregulation be sustained? And the answer largely depends on whether carriers can continue to maintain the benefits in the face of the industry's poor financial performance during the past few years or whether they will be able to appropriate these benefits to maintain their basic viability.

Airlines could appropriate the benefits of deregulation to themselves in at least three ways. First, they could hinder competition in their markets and then raise fares. One possible impediment to competition is that any carrier that might wish to compete on routes connected to another carrier's major hubs would have to enter the market on a large scale to match its competitor's large number of flights on those routes. Another impediment is the frequent flier programs that reward passengers for past patronage and encourage continued patronage by giving them free trips to domestic and international destinations served by the carrier. A final possible barrier to competition is computer reservation systems. The carrier that owns a system has a potential competitive edge because it is easier for travel agents who use the system to obtain information about that carrier's flights.

With fewer effective competitors at the national level, carriers could find it easier to establish a cooperative arrangement that enables them to maintain fare increases and to avoid fare wars. Finally, travel restrictions already attached to discount fares could be tightened, forcing losses on travelers from higher (unrestricted) fares or greater service inconvenience. These issues will be examined in chapter 4.

Airline profits have continued to be cyclical, yet rarely during deregulation have they exceeded a normal return. In the past few years the industry has lost billions of dollars. This situation has prompted three classes of questions. What explains the large losses? What type of carriers—national, regional, commuter—will survive the slump? And is the only industry structure that is viable in the long run less competitive than the current structure? These questions are addressed in chapters 5 and 6. Finally, in chapter 7 we assess whether policymakers will need to become more active in mediating the interests of travelers and carriers.

Appendix

This appendix estimates the net effect on travelers' welfare of fewer interline connections but in the context of more connections overall. To obtain this estimate, we performed calculations based on the number of passengers taking one-way trips with two or fewer segments and round-trips with two or fewer segments on the outbound and return legs (the same data used in figure 2-9). Following this procedure reduced the likelihood that intermediate destinations were improperly viewed as points of connection because the data did not allow one to distinguish between a connection and an intermediate destination.

To estimate the benefits of fewer interline connections, we calculated the percentage of connections from the first three quarters of 1978 that were interline. This percentage was multiplied by the percentage of connecting passengers to yield an estimate of the percentage of passengers who would have had interline connections if regulation had continued. We subtracted the actual percentage of passengers making interline connections from this figure to yield the percentage of passengers who now have on-line connections but would have had interline connections if regulation had continued. This resulting figure was multiplied by the number of passengers involved to obtain, for a given quarter, an estimate of the reduction in the number of interline connections due to deregulation. Multiplying this estimated reduction by $37 (the value of an on-line versus an interline connection reported in note 17) and averaging over the period 1979–93 gave an estimate of the average annual benefit to travelers from fewer interline connections of $0.85 billion in 1993 dollars.

To estimate the cost of additional connections, we calculated the percentage of travelers from the first three quarters of 1978 to estimate the percentage of connecting passengers under regulation. This figure was subtracted from the actual percentage of connecting passengers to yield the additional percentage of connecting passengers under deregulation. This additional percentage was multiplied by the number of passengers involved to give the number of extra connecting passengers. Based on findings in Steven A. Morrison and Clifford Winston, "Enhancing the Performance of the Deregulated Air Transportation System," *Brookings Papers on Economic Activity: Microeconomics* (1989), pp. 61–112, and assuming a 1,500 mile trip distance, an additional connection adds 66 minutes of transfer time and an additional 65 minutes to travel time. Based on the values of travel and transfer time obtained by Morrison and Winston, the average annual cost of additional connections is $0.69 billion in 1993 dollars. Because these calculations involved a subset of all passengers, both figures are understated, but their difference, approximately zero, should be reasonably accurate.

PART TWO

Analysis

CHAPTER THREE

Organizational and Methodological Overview

FROM a research perspective the subjects raised in chapter 2 translate into a series of empirical vignettes, which we have organized into traveler and carrier studies. Most issues in the airline industry, of course, have implications for both travelers and carriers, but we have framed our studies according to how the subjects have appeared in the public debate. Thus although impediments to competition, pricing cooperation, and travel restrictions obviously affect carrier profitability, they are treated in chapter 4 as travelers' issues because of policymakers' concerns that they could lead to higher fares and less convenient service. Similarly, although the quality of managerial decisions and the particular airlines that compete in individual markets affect the fares and service that travelers receive, they are treated in chapter 5 as carriers' issues because they would seem to have a critical effect on carrier profitability.

Because most of the vignettes represent a first attempt at empirically analyzing a particular matter over time, the results cannot be compared to earlier studies. In a few instances we have identified previous work that corroborates our initial findings and then have extended the time period of the analysis. Another point to bear in mind is that because of the diversity of the issues we have addressed, we have not been able to draw upon or develop a comprehensive analytical framework that could guide all our analyses.

One theme that emerges in several studies, however, is how various aspects of competition affect fares. An analytical tool used briefly in chapter 2 and used again extensively to address the effects of competition on fares is called a *fare equation*. Beginning with the work of Elizabeth E. Bailey and John C. Panzar in 1981, a large literature has developed that estimates the impact of airline competition on deregulated fares.[1]

---

1. See Elizabeth E. Bailey and John C. Panzar, "The Contestability of Airline Markets during the Transition to Deregulation," *Law and Contemporary Problems*, vol. 44 (Winter

In the most basic form of this equation, fares, usually an average fare on a route, have been determined by actual and potential airline competition, the length of the route, and traffic density.[2] Length and density take into account the influence of cost and demand. Actual competitors are carriers that serve the route, and potential competitors are those operating at the airports that make up the route and, by their very presence, may constrain incumbent carriers' behavior.[3]

We present illustrative estimates of a basic fare equation for the third quarter of 1993 based on quarterly data for each carrier providing direct (same plane) or on-line (same carrier) connecting service on the 1,000 most heavily traveled domestic routes (as measured in 1990).[4] All varia-

---

1981), pp. 125–45. Other analyses using fare equations include David R. Graham, Daniel P. Kaplan, and David S. Sibley, "Efficiency and Competition in the Airline Industry," *Bell Journal of Economics*, vol. 14 (Spring 1983), pp. 118–38; Gregory D. Call and Theodore E. Keeler, "Airline Deregulation, Fares, and Market Behavior: Some Empirical Evidence," in Andrew F. Daughety, ed., *Analytical Studies in Transport Economics* (Cambridge University Press, 1985), pp. 221–48; Elizabeth E. Bailey, David R. Graham, and Daniel P. Kaplan, *Deregulating the Airlines* (MIT Press, 1985); Steven A. Morrison and Clifford Winston, "Empirical Implications and Tests of the Contestability Hypothesis," *Journal of Law and Economics*, vol. 30 (April 1987), pp. 53–66; Severin Borenstein, "Hubs and High Fares: Dominance and Market Power in the U.S. Airline Industry," *Rand Journal of Economics*, vol. 20 (Autumn 1989), pp. 344–65; Gloria J. Hurdle and others, "Concentration, Potential Entry, and Performance in the Airline Industry," *Journal of Industrial Economics*, vol. 38 (December 1989), pp. 119–39; Diana L. Strassman, "Potential Competition in the Deregulated Airline Industry," *Review of Economics and Statistics*, vol. 72 (November 1990), pp. 696–702; Steven A. Morrison and Clifford Winston, "The Dynamics of Airline Pricing and Competition," *American Economic Review*, vol. 80 (May 1990), pp. 389–93; Jan K. Brueckner, Nichola T. Dyer, and Pablo T. Spiller, "Fare Determination in Airline Hub-and-Spoke Networks," *Rand Journal of Economics*, vol. 23 (Autumn 1992), pp. 309–33; Jan K. Brueckner and Pablo T. Spiller, "Economies of Traffic Density in the Deregulated Airline Industry," *Journal of Law and Economics*, vol. 37 (October 1994), pp. 379–415; Margaret A. Peteraf and Randal Reed, "Pricing and Performance in Monopoly Airline Markets," *Journal of Law and Economics*, vol. 37 (April 1994), pp. 193–213; and William N. Evans and Ioannis N. Kessides, "Living by the 'Golden Rule': Multimarket Contact in the U.S. Airline Industry," *Quarterly Journal of Economics*, vol. 109 (May 1994), pp. 341–66.

2. More complex specifications of fare equations typically begin with this specification and then proceed to include additional measures of airline competition (see, for example, Evans and Kessides, "Living by the 'Golden Rule'").

3. The distinction between actual and potential competitors emerged from the theory of contestable markets, which posits that if entry and exit by potential competitors is costless, the incumbent firm's behavior is constrained so that prices maximize market welfare. See William J. Baumol, John C. Panzar, and Robert D. Willig, *Contestable Markets and the Theory of Industrial Structure* (Harcourt Brace Jovanovich, 1982).

4. For this simple illustrative estimation we have treated the competition measures and passengers as exogenous. There has been an unresolved debate about the appropriateness of treating these variables, especially the competition measures, as exogenous in fare

bles, including the dependent variable, have been measured in natural logarithms. The estimated equation also includes a constant term and dummy variables for each of the ten largest carriers in 1993.[5] The airline dummies are statistically significantly different from one another, indicating that airlines' fare policies differ. The estimated coefficients are as follows, with heteroskedastic-consistent standard errors in parentheses:

$$\ln\ (average\ fare)\ =\ -\ 0.027\ \ln\ (route\ competitors)$$
$$(0.013)$$

$$-\ 0.120\ \ln\ (airport\ competitors)$$
$$(0.010)$$

$$+\ 0.383\ \ln\ (distance)$$
$$(0.008)$$

$$-\ 0.048\ \ln\ (route\ passengers)$$
$$(0.005)$$

$$R^2\ =\ 0.48;\ N\ =\ 5{,}513.$$

The findings are broadly similar to those in other studies that have used a comparable sample.[6] Fares increase with distance, although less than proportionally because of the fixed costs of takeoff and landing. An increase in the number of route competitors (the number of effective

---

regressions. For example, Bailey, Graham, and Kaplan, *Deregulating the Airlines*, presented statistical tests that did not reject exogeneity, while Call and Keeler, "Airline Deregulation, Fares, and Market Behavior," also argued that competition should be treated as exogenous and not jointly determined with fares. But other researchers such as Peteraf and Reed, "Pricing and Performance in Monopoly Airline Markets," have statistically rejected exogeneity. The difficulty in resolving the debate is that concerns have been raised that the statistical tests, regardless of their outcome, have low power. The approach we have taken toward this issue has been to indicate, where appropriate, how exogeneity concerns bear on our central findings. When we used a disaggregate measure of airline competition (dummy variables to identify the effect of individual carriers on fares), our findings were not materially affected by whether these dummy variables were treated as exogenous or endogenous.

Passenger flows on most routes are highly correlated with the populations at the metropolitan areas that make up the route. A simultaneous change in fares across routes could influence passenger flows by generating additional trips on some routes and by causing a shift in destinations for pleasure travelers. We therefore used the populations at the metropolitan areas that make up the route as an alternative and a truly exogenous control for traffic density and routinely found that our conclusions were not influenced by whether we used route passengers or metropolitan area populations in the fare equations.

5. Data are from the Department of Transportation Data Bank 1A.

6. See, for example, Borenstein, "Hubs and High Fares"; and Morrison and Winston, "Dynamics of Airline Pricing and Competition."

competitors on the route) and the number of airport competitors (the minimum number of effective competitors at the route's endpoints) reduces fares. Finally, increases in route density (the number of passengers on the route) also cause fares to fall.

We have extended this basic equation in a number of different directions. In chapter 4, we have extended the baseline specification to control for behavior that we have interpreted as price leadership (in which a carrier proposes a fare change, sees if other carriers follow, then reacts accordingly), thus enabling us to estimate the effect of price leadership on fare-cost margins. In chapters 5 and 6 we have included more disaggregated measures of competitors on the route. One specification included bankrupt carriers on a route and has enabled us to estimate the cost to other carriers of competing with them. Another specification included the percentage of a carrier's revenue earned in markets where it competes with one other particular carrier, which allowed us to estimate the effects of multimarket contact on a carrier's fares. A final specification included dummy variables indicating whether a particular carrier serves a route, which enabled us to estimate the effect a particular carrier has on all other carriers' fares. Throughout the fare estimations we have typically focused on a few key variables, using relatively simple but appropriate specifications of the background variables to control for other influences and presenting sensitivity tests of our findings in appendixes.

CHAPTER FOUR

Airline Behavior and Traveler Welfare

FACED WITH the challenge of maximizing profits without the protection of economic regulation, air carriers dramatically changed their operations, pricing, and service even before formal deregulation began in October 1978. When deregulation began, few economists envisioned any serious impediments to airline competition. Indeed, some thought air transport was clearly a contestable market.[1] But as the industry has evolved and carriers have become accustomed to the new rules, even strong supporters of deregulation have become concerned that airlines are discovering ways to minimize the effects of competition, thus enabling them to capture gains that accrued to travelers from deregulation. This concern, however, has little empirical foundation: travelers continue to enjoy substantial benefits from deregulation.

Impediments to Competition

Carriers were not passive in the face of competition unleashed by deregulation. Some, notably American and United Airlines, developed marketing and operating strategies, including frequent flier programs, computer reservation systems, and additional hubs, to give them a competitive edge over their rivals. Naturally, other large carriers responded with the same strategies. Thus the question has arisen as to whether some carriers, because of their rivals' size or network characteristics, face competitive disadvantages unrelated to efficiency or service differences

---

1. See, for example, Elizabeth E. Bailey and William J. Baumol, "Deregulation and the Theory of Contestable Markets," *Yale Journal on Regulation*, vol. 1, no. 2 (1984), pp. 111–28. Contestable markets theory, which stresses the importance of potential competitors in disciplining the pricing behavior of firms already in a market, was used to provide retrospective support for deregulation during the early 1980s and prospective support for several proposed mergers during the mid-1980s.

and whether the advantaged carriers are able to raise fares without significantly losing their market shares.

Hubs and Fares

One controversial source of differences in fares has been the hub-and-spoke route system. Although the system originated under regulation, it often forced customers to change airlines as well as planes at a hub. The system grew swiftly under deregulation, which, by eliminating restrictions on carriers' choice to enter or exit markets, allowed them to feed themselves connecting passengers (on-line connections) at existing hubs and to establish new hubs. Hub-and-spoke systems were designed to decrease carrier costs by centralizing planning and maintenance, and by filling planes closer to capacity because people can be gathered from many places, sorted out at the hub with timely connecting flights, and sent on to many other places. By offering more connections between cities, the systems also increased flight frequencies for travelers. At a typical hub, more than half the passengers boarding planes are in midroute rather than beginning a trip. In 1993, for example, 56 percent of passenger boardings at Chicago's O'Hare Airport were making connecting flights. Figures for Dallas–Fort Worth, Atlanta, and Denver were 66 percent, 64 percent, and 57 percent, respectively. Charlotte topped the list with 77 percent of boardings from connections.[2]

Because interline connections have all but disappeared, these figures indicate that hub airports are likely to be dominated by one or two airlines (table 4-1).[3] What effect does this dominance have on the fares

2. These figures were calculated by the authors from Department of Transportation Data Bank 1A, the 10 percent ticket sample.

3. These fifteen airports were used by the General Accounting Office in a study of fares at concentrated hub airports. See *Airline Competition: Higher Fares and Reduced Competition at Concentrated Airports*, GAO/RCED 90-102 (July 1990), p. 15. To be included in the "concentrated" category, an airport had to be one of the busiest seventy-five airports in the country based on enplanements and had to have one airline enplaning at least 60 percent of the passengers or two airlines together accounting for at least 85 percent. Airports that met this first criterion but that were in metropolitan areas that were served by more than one major commercial airport (Baltimore-Washington, Chicago, Dallas, Houston, Los Angeles, New York, and San Francisco, for example) were excluded because a carrier's dominance of a single airport is a misleading fact when travelers have a choice of airports. Some airports in table 4-1 no longer meet the GAO's definition of concentrated. This illustrates the changing nature of the airline industry.

Table 4-1. *Share of Enplanements of the Dominant Carrier at Concentrated Hub Airports, 1978, 1993*
Percent

	1978		1993	
Airport	*Share*	*Carrier*	*Share*	*Carrier*
Atlanta	49.7	Delta	83.5	Delta
Charlotte	74.8	Eastern	94.6	USAir
Cincinnati	35.1	Delta	89.8	Delta
Dayton	35.3	TWA	40.5	USAir
Denver	32.0	United	51.8	United
Detroit	21.7	American	74.8	Northwest
Greensboro	64.5	Eastern	44.9	USAir
Memphis	42.2	Delta	76.3	Northwest
Minneapolis–St. Paul	31.7	Northwest	80.6	Northwest
Nashville	28.5	American	69.8	American
Pittsburgh	46.7	Allegheny	88.9	USAir
Raleigh-Durham	74.2	Eastern	80.4	American
St. Louis	39.4	TWA	60.4	TWA
Salt Lake City	39.6	Western	71.4	Delta
Syracuse	40.5	Allegheny	49.5	USAir

Source: Authors' calculations from enplanement data in Federal Aviation Adminstration, *Airport Activity Statistics of the Certificated Route Air Carriers* (Department of Transportation, various years).

paid by travelers who begin their trips at one of the hubs?[4] This question has been addressed in different ways by academics and policy analysts. Because academics seek to understand the sources of competition in airline markets, they estimate a fare equation to identify the independent effect of various measures of airline competition on fares. A frequent finding has been that airport dominance (measured, for example, by a carrier's percentage of passenger originations at an airport) increases fares.[5] That is, as the baseline fare equation in chapter 3 showed, competition in airline markets occurs not only on routes but also at airports.

4. Travelers who begin or end their trips elsewhere and only change planes at the hub are in a different situation because of competition among hubs. For example, a person traveling on a connecting flight from Boston to Los Angeles could choose to connect in Chicago (on American or United), Dallas (on American or Delta), Minneapolis (on Northwest), Pittsburgh (on USAir), or St. Louis (on TWA), among other airports.

5. See, for example, Severin Borenstein, "Hubs and High Fares: Dominance and Market Power in the U.S. Airline Industry," *Rand Journal of Economics*, vol. 20 (Autumn 1989), pp. 344–65.

Policy analysts, building on the findings of the academics, have approached the problem from the travelers' perspective and asked whether fares for trips that originate at dominant hub airports are high enough relative to fares for trips that originate at other airports to warrant policy intervention.[6] The goal of their studies has not been to measure the effect of individual variables on airfares but to measure the collective effect of all influences on fares at dominant hub airports relative to their effect on fares at a control group of airports. Here, a fare equation is not needed. Ideally, fares from the dominant airports would be compared with fares for identical trips from the control group of airports. The size of the difference would measure the extent, if any, of the problem.

In a 1990 study widely cited in the press, the General Accounting Office found that in 1988, yield (average fare per mile) for trips originating at fifteen hub airports dominated by one or two carriers was 27 percent higher than yield at thirty-eight unconcentrated airports used as a control group.[7] But by merely comparing yields, the GAO in effect assumed that the trips taken from the two groups of airports were identical. An accurate comparison of yields, however, requires taking into account route distance, number of plane changes, traffic mix, carrier identity, and frequent flier tickets.

Yield falls as distance increases because the costs of takeoff and landing are fixed. And because routes with a hub at one or both endpoints have shorter average trip distances than other routes, failure to account for distance will make flights using hubs appear to be more expensive than they are. Trips requiring a change of planes have lower fares than single-plane flights because passengers consider changing planes less desirable than taking a nonstop flight. Again, because hubs have a greater proportion of nonstop flights than nonhubs, not correcting for plane changes would also make the fare premium for flights out of hubs appear larger than it is. The mix of fares must be taken into account because a larger proportion of full-fare tickets relative to discount tickets at a given airport would affect yield comparisons. Carrier identity must be considered: a carrier might charge high fares at a hub (Delta at Atlanta, for instance) because it charges high fares at all the airports it serves. Finally,

6. See, for example, General Accounting Office, *Airline Competition*.
7. See General Accounting Office, *Airline Competition*, p. 3. The thirty-eight unconcentrated airports were in the forty-eight contiguous states, were among the top seventy-five airports in the country based on enplanements, did not meet the GAO's definition of a concentrated airport, and were not in multiairport cities.

because yields are higher on routes with more frequent fliers, it is necessary to include in the yield calculation the passengers who fly free
because they are using their frequent flier awards.[8] Frequent fliers are
also likely to constitute a larger share of passengers at hub airports, so
excluding them from the analysis would inappropriately inflate hub yields
relative to nonhub yields.[9]

Here we present the results of an analysis using, as did the GAO, a
control group of airports, but adjusting also for the five factors we have
mentioned. Frequent flier tickets were included in the calculations. To
control for traffic mix, we used twenty-seven of the GAO's control group
of thirty-eight airports, excluding eleven located in Florida, Arizona,
California, and Nevada that were likely to have a greater proportion of
tourist traffic than the concentrated airports. Our yield comparison took
account of distance, number of plane changes, and carrier identity by
first using all the trips from the control group of twenty-seven unconcentrated airports to calculate the yield for 100-mile distance bands, trips
with no plane change and one change, and each carrier.[10] We then calculated what the fare for each trip from the concentrated airports would
be if its price were based on the yield for a comparable trip from the
unconcentrated control group. The fare premium was the percentage by
which actual revenue at the concentrated airports exceeded the revenue
that would have been collected had airlines used the same pricing scheme
at concentrated and unconcentrated airports.

The estimates obtained from our adjusted hub premium compared
with the premium based on the GAO's unadjusted methodology from
the fourth quarter of 1978 to the fourth quarter of 1993 are shown in

8. See Steven A. Morrison and Clifford Winston, "Enhancing the Performance of the
Deregulated Air Transportation System," *Brookings Papers on Economic Activity: Microeconomics* (1989), pp. 61–123.

9. See Michael E. Levine, "Airline Competition in Deregulated Markets: Theory, Firm
Strategy, and Public Policy," *Yale Journal on Regulation*, vol. 4 (Spring 1987), pp. 393–494.

10. Although the GAO stresses its uncorrected results, it did make a crude correction
for distance by comparing yields at the fifteen concentrated airports with yields at twenty-
two unconcentrated airports (a subset of the thirty-eight) that had comparable average trip
distances. But because the fare-distance relationship is nonlinear, two airports with identical
average trip distances will have different yields, even in the absence of any "premium," if
the distribution of trip distances differs. For example, suppose the fare-distance relationship
at two airports is $F = AD^{0.5}$ (where F is fare, D is distance, and A is a constant). For one
airport, half the trips are 500 miles, the other half are 1,500 miles. At the other airport,
all trips are 1,000 miles. Both airports have an average trip distance of 1,000 miles, but
the first airport has an average fare 3.5 percent lower than the other airport because
$(500^{0.5} + 1,500^{0.5})/2$ is 3.5 percent lower than $1,000^{0.5}$

Figure 4-1.   *Yield Premiums at Fifteen Concentrated Hub Airports
under Two Methods of Determination, 1978–93*

Percent

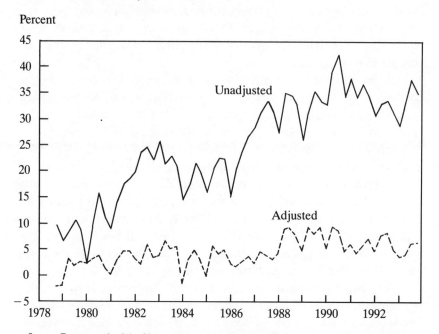

Source: Fares at each of the fifteen concentrated airports studied by the General Accounting Office
are from a subsample of the Department of Transportation's 10 percent sample of airline tickets (Data
Bank 1A). This subsample was all domestic round-trip tickets with two or fewer segments outbound
and two or fewer segments return. See text for more details.

figure 4-1. Although there is a hub premium, it is much smaller than the
GAO figure. The premium peaked in 1988–90 at nearly 10 percent and
has since fallen by 4 to 7 percent. For 1993 it amounted to $240 million
in additional fare revenue, or less than 2 percent of the $12.4 billion
in travelers' benefits from the lower deregulated fares reported in
chapter 2.[11]

For 1993 the GAO's unadjusted methodology gives a hub premium of
33.4 percent. Our method gives 5.2 percent, a difference of 28.2 percentage points. The factors accounting for most of the difference are our
corrections for distance and number of plane changes, which together
account for 18.6 percentage points (66 percent of the difference). Using

11. Using Data Bank 1A, we calculated that during 1993 originating enplanements at
the fifteen GAO concentrated airports accounted for 9.8 percent of total U.S. enplanements. Using an average hub premium of 5 percent and $48.7 billion in domestic passenger
revenue yields the figure in the text.

carrier-specific comparisons accounts for 4.6 percentage points (16 percent of the difference). Correcting for frequent flier programs accounts for 2.5 percentage points (9 percent of the difference), as does excluding the California, Arizona, Nevada, and Florida comparison airports.[12] The hub premium is so small, relative to the fare reductions from deregulation, that travelers to and from concentrated hubs still pay less than they would have under regulation.

Frequent Flier Programs

Airlines compete in many ways—price, service quality, advertising, and promotions. Under regulation, when fare competition was not allowed, carriers competed excessively in service quality, particularly flight frequency. Although deregulation enabled them to compete on fares and use discounts to fill up planes, airlines continue to compete in flight frequency. Indeed, frequency has increased because the hub-and-spoke systems offer more connections between cities. And airlines have also developed promotions, particularly frequent flier programs, to attract passengers.

A frequent flier program could give a large airline that serves many cities, including attractive vacation destinations, a competitive advantage over carriers with smaller networks, an advantage unrelated to any efficiency or service characteristics of the larger airline. Indeed, it has been claimed that frequent flier programs were invented to impede market entry.[13] We estimated the effect that frequent flier programs have on carriers' market shares by developing a model of how people make choices among airlines.[14]

12. In a subsequent study, *Airline Competition: Higher Fares and Less Competition Continue at Concentrated Airports*, GAO/RCED 93-171 (July 1993), the GAO, using earlier drafts of this chapter, partially adopted our methodology. They controlled for distance and frequent flier miles but not for carrier identity or traffic mix, and they only partially corrected for number of plane changes. Their results for the year ending after the first quarter of 1993 were that yield was 19.8 percent higher at concentrated airports (p. 10). Considering the relative importance of the various correction factors, had they corrected for all of the factors that we did, they would have found a modest hub premium consistent with our finding. We cannot compare our findings with those obtained in academic studies because they use a regression framework that holds certain influences constant that we needed to adjust to calculate a hub premium.

13. See Levine, "Airline Competition in Deregulated Markets," pp. 393–494.

14. This model was based on and extends the airline choice model in Morrison and Winston, "Enhancing the Performance of the Deregulated Air Transportation System."

Our model assumed that each passenger chooses the carrier and routing (for example, American Airlines, nonstop) that maximizes his or her utility. The choice is influenced by each carrier's fare, service quality, promotions, loyalty, and reputation. The fare class (coach or discount, for example) was assumed to be given, and we used the average fare for the chosen class and routing; higher fares should decrease the likelihood of a carrier's being selected.[15] The dimensions of service quality included for each carrier and routing were the average number of daily departures and the scheduled travel time, including connecting time when required.[16] More frequent daily departures by a given airline should influence travelers to choose it; greater travel time should have a negative influence. Promotions were reflected by available frequent flier mileage for a given trip, based on trip distance.[17] We multiplied available frequent flier mileage with the number of cities a carrier serves in order to capture the convenience and promotional aspects of a carrier's network. That is, the more cities served, the more valuable a frequent flier mile. Because eligibility for free trips occurs at discrete levels of mileage accumulation, we allowed available frequent flier mileage for a trip to have different effects, depending on the mileage a traveler had accumulated in each

---

Previous aggregate models of airline demand have included James E. Anderson and Marvin Kraus, "Quality of Service and the Demand for Air Travel," *Review of Economics and Statistics*, vol. 63 (November 1981), pp. 533–40; and Arthur De Vany, "The Revealed Value of Time in Air Travel," *Review of Economics and Statistics*, vol. 56 (February 1974), pp. 77–82.

15. Attempts to treat fare class as endogenous, using a fare class choice model, were unsuccessful. We attempted to estimate a nested logit model in which the upper nest was the choice of a restricted or unrestricted ticket and the lower nest was the choice of carrier. Given this structure, the effect of fare on fare class choice would be captured in the log sum (expected utility) from the carrier choice model. Problems arose because we were unable to estimate a separate carrier choice model for unrestricted travelers because of an insufficient number of observations. The implications of maintaining fare class exogeneity, we have argued in "Enhancing the Performance of the Deregulated Air Transportation System," are probably minor given our primary interest in the effects of frequent flier programs on market shares. Another choice that was not modeled, the choice of whether to travel, has even less relevance to this analysis.

16. Other possible service variables, including on-time performance, number of complaints to the Department of Transportation, and safety records, were statistically insignificant. We also investigated other service-time variables and specifications such as a separate transfer time variable, connection dummies, and so on, but these did not lead to improvements in the model.

17. The number of miles awarded for a given trip may be different from trip distance because of various promotions. Although it is difficult to account for these accurately, they probably apply to only a minority of travelers.

carrier's program.[18] We also allowed available frequent flier mileage for a trip to have different effects according to whether the traveler or someone else paid for the ticket. Frequent flier mileage multiplied by the number of cities served should favorably influence a traveler's choice of carrier.[19]

Drawing on marketing literature, we interpreted carrier loyalty as consumers' tendency to use the same airline based on cumulative experiences with that airline, independent of other influences on airline choice.[20] The effect of carrier loyalty, that is, a traveler's accumulated information about an airline, was measured by the number of trips he or she has taken on that airline.[21] Carrier loyalty should influence a traveler to choose a given carrier. Finally, because we controlled for flight frequency, the effects of reputation were captured by a hub dummy equal

18. It is most likely that our sample captured a representative stage of mileage accumulation for the traveling public, many of whom are members of more than one frequent flier program. That is, some air travelers in our sample may have just redeemed their miles and others may have been just about to do so, but on average accumulations should not have been biased in any particular direction. Thus our simulations should be representative of the traveling public's mileage accumulation on individual carriers. The categories we used were 0–3,500 miles, 3,501–15,000 miles, 15,001–80,000 miles, and more than 80,000 miles. The first interval represents an infrequent traveler (less than one transcontinental trip) or one who has just redeemed his miles. The second represents a traveler possibly within one transcontinental trip for an award (during our sample period many carriers offered a free trip in the continental United States for 20,000 miles). The third represents a traveler who is possibly within any type of trip for an award. The final interval represents a traveler who has accumulated at least enough mileage for two free coach trips to Europe. These intervals are also consistent with the miles needed to upgrade to a higher class of service. Results were not particularly sensitive to changes in these intervals. We were unable to specify different frequent flier parameters for each carrier because of insufficient degrees of freedom.

19. We investigated nonlinear specifications of the interaction between frequent flier mileage and cities served to determine whether the marginal value of a frequent flier mile increased more than, less than, or the same as an increase in the number of cities served (and vice versa). We found that the value of the log likelihood at convergence was maximized using the linear interaction specification; that is, the marginal value of a mile increased the same as an increase in the number of cities served.

20. This idea of loyalty was discussed in the context of automobiles by Fred Mannering and Clifford Winston, "Brand Loyalty and the Decline of American Automobile Firms," *Brookings Papers on Economic Activity: Microeconomics* (1991), pp. 67–114.

21. The effect of loyalty is probably most important and easiest for survey respondents to construct for relatively recent travel experience. Thus we used the number of trips taken during a traveler's current accumulation of frequent flier miles on a given carrier. We explored alternative functional forms for this variable, including nonlinear specifications, but as in the case in Mannering and Winston, "Brand Loyalty," we found that the best statistical fits were obtained with a simple linear specification of the loyalty variable.

to 1 if the carrier in question has a hub at the origin and airline dummy variables (Alaska and Midway Air's dummies were set to zero). Airlines that have hubs at a passenger's origin enhance their reputations and increase the likelihood that travelers will select them. Airline preference dummy variables capture the tendency for travelers to select a specific carrier, all else equal.[22]

To estimate the parameters of our model, we commissioned a survey of air passenger round-trips with a single destination taken during June, November, or December 1990. From the survey we identified each traveler's carrier and routing choice and then, using the *Official Airline Guide*, determined all possible carrier and routing alternatives the traveler could have chosen.[23]

To represent air travelers' choices, we used a multinomial logit model, commonly used to estimate the relative importance of influences on a discrete choice such as the choice of airline and routing.[24] Our interest in the parameter estimates presented in table 4-2 was to find out what value travelers place on the various aspects of flying on different carriers. The coefficients have their expected signs and, in general, have been

22. The preference dummies could also have been capturing omitted variables. Note that carrier preference is distinct from carrier loyalty, which is based on cumulative carrier experience.

23. The sample was based on a diary survey using a national household panel managed by Allison-Fisher, Inc., and administered by National Family Opinion, Inc., Toledo, Ohio. The diary included a traveler's carrier choice, routing, information on frequent flier memberships and accumulated unspent mileage, and who paid for the ticket. The final sample consisted of 169 round-trips (direct and connecting) covering 146 markets.

24. The multinomial logit choice probabilities are given by

$$Prob_i = \exp(\beta X_i) / \sum_{j=1}^{J} \exp(\beta X_j),$$

where $Prob_i$ is the probability of selecting airline-routing alternative i, parameters are denoted by β, explanatory variables denoted by X, and J is the set of carrier-routing alternatives including alternative i. As in Morrison and Winston, "Enhancing the Performance of the Deregulated Air Transportation System," we followed standard practice and subsampled all the available carrier and routing alternatives to construct choice sets for estimation purposes. We also could not reject the multinomial logit specification, in particular the independence of irrelevant alternatives (IIA) assumption, at high levels of confidence. Our sample contained more than one trip by the same traveler in some instances, which could lead to biased or inefficient estimates because error terms from the same traveler may be correlated. To examine the extent of the bias, we fitted models using only one random trip from each traveler. Estimation of these models produced results that were very close to the models in which repeat observations were included. Thus the bias, if any, from including repeat observations here appears to be small.

precisely estimated. The frequent flier mileage coefficients were especially important to our analysis.[25] Consider first those travelers who buy their own ticket. Estimates indicate that their valuation of additional frequent flier miles is aligned with carriers' award schedules. Travelers who fly infrequently and have accumulated little mileage and those who fly often and have accumulated a lot of miles place a statistically insignificant value on additional mileage. But travelers who have accumulated almost enough miles for a free trip place a very high value on additional mileage. The marginal value of an additional mile for travelers who have accumulated 3,501 to 15,000 miles is 13.0 cents, and the marginal value for travelers who have accumulated 15,001 to 80,000 miles is 21.5 cents.[26] The marginal value averaged over all mileage accumulation levels, obtained by restricting the four frequent flier mileage coefficients to be equal, is 8.2 cents. (This value is later used for purposes of sensitivity testing in our simulations.)

To our knowledge there are no other estimates with which to compare these results to assess their accuracy, and economic theory can provide only limited guidance in making such an assessment. That is, although constrained utility-maximizing behavior would lead travelers to value miles on the margin at their market value, it is likely that their actual valuations would sharply deviate from the theoretical equality for two reasons. First, travelers are forced to make "purchases" of frequent flier miles equal to the number of miles of their round-trip. Thus these purchases cannot be continuously adjusted to maximize utility.[27] Second, if people would like to travel more than they do but cannot because they do not have enough time, the simple theoretical equality of their valuation of miles and the market's valuation need not hold; the time con-

---

25. We conducted a suggestive test of the endogeneity of cumulative miles, which was used to construct the frequent flier variable, and the endogeneity of previous trips by instrumenting these variables and using the predicted frequent flier and trips variables instead of the actual variables in the choice models. The instruments were traveler characteristics such as income, age, occupation, home ownership, frequent flier membership status, and so on and carrier characteristics such as hubs and frequency. The coefficients of the predicted variables were only slightly higher than the coefficients of the actual variables, and other variables were unaffected. Thus we used the actual variables in our final estimation.

26. These estimates are the ratio of the appropriate miles awarded-cities served coefficient and the fare coefficient, based on an average of ninety-five cities served.

27. There are undoubtedly some travelers who optimize on the margin by participating in markets where frequent flier miles are bought and sold.

Table 4-2. *Airline Choice Model Estimates*[a]

Explanatory variable	Coefficient[b]
Average fare for chosen fare class (dollars)	−0.0069
	(0.0014)
Travel time (minutes)	−0.00055
	(0.00008)
Average daily departures	0.2440
	(0.0588)
Frequent flier miles awarded times number of cities (domestic and foreign) served by carrier if traveler paid for the ticket and has accumulated frequent flier mileage between 0 and 3,500 miles; 0 otherwise (thousands)	0.0030 (0.0051)
Frequent flier miles awarded times number of cities (domestic and foreign) served by carrier if traveler paid for the ticket and has accumulated frequent flier mileage between 3,501 and 15,000 miles; 0 otherwise (thousands)	0.0095 (0.0038)
Frequent flier miles awarded times number of cities (domestic and foreign) served by carrier if traveler paid for the ticket and has accumulated frequent flier mileage between 15,001 and 80,000 miles; 0 otherwise (thousands)	0.0156 (0.0045)
Frequent flier miles awarded times number of cities (domestic and foreign) served by carrier if traveler paid for the ticket and has accumulated frequent flier mileage greater than 80,000 miles; 0 otherwise (thousands)	−0.0055 (0.0132)
Frequent flier miles awarded times number of cities (domestic and foreign) served by carrier if someone else paid for the traveler's ticket; 0 otherwise (thousands)	0.0122 (0.0028)
Cumulative number of trips taken by traveler during current accumulation of frequent flier miles, defined for largest 8 carriers (American, United, Delta, USAir, Continental, Northwest, TWA, Eastern); 0 otherwise	0.0081 (0.0042)

straint prevents a person from traveling enough to bring the value he or she places on frequent flier miles down to the market valuation.

Additional considerations suggest the high valuations are reasonable. From a statistical perspective, it seems unlikely that omitted variables could lead to inflated values for two of the frequent flier award coefficients but not affect the other two, whose statistical insignificance is quite plausible. From a behavioral perspective, a traveler who has accumulated 19,000 miles on United Airlines, for instance, and faces a choice of carriers for a round-trip of 1,000 miles would undoubtedly be willing to pay a much higher fare for a United flight to get the additional 1,000 miles, which, by giving him enough for a free trip, would add substantial value to his entire stock of miles. A free trip could also expand travel

Explanatory variable	Coefficient[b]
Cumulative number of trips taken by traveler during current accumulation of frequent flier miles, defined for smallest 4 carriers (America West, Southwest, Midway, Alaska); 0 otherwise	0.0414 (0.0278)
Hub dummy (1 if origin is carrier's hub; 0 otherwise)	0.2204 (0.3742)
American dummy[c] (1 if American Airlines, 0 otherwise)	−2.462 (0.407)
United dummy[c] (1 if United Airlines, 0 otherwise)	−1.266 (0.378)
Delta dummy[c] (1 if Delta Airlines, 0 otherwise)	−2.022 (0.358)
Continental dummy[c] (1 if Continental Airlines, 0 otherwise)	−1.006 (0.426)
USAir dummy[c] (1 if USAir, 0 otherwise)	−1.634 (0.420)
Southwest dummy[c] (1 if Southwest Airlines, 0 otherwise)	−2.694 (0.635)
Northwest dummy[c] (1 if Northwest Airlines, 0 otherwise)	−1.077 (0.455)
TWA dummy[c] (1 if TWA, 0 otherwise)	−1.604 (0.543)
Eastern dummy[c] (1 if Eastern Airlines, 0 otherwise)	−1.901 (0.651)
America West dummy[c] (1 if America West Airlines, 0 otherwise)	−2.101 (0.803)

Sources: Restricted or discount fares are unpublished data from the Airline Tariff Publishing Company. Unrestricted (coach) fares, travel times, and average daily departures are from *Official Airline Guide* (June, November, December 1990). Airlines' cities served are from the Department of Transportation, *Airport Activity Statistics of Certificated Route Air Carriers* (1990). Airlines provided information on their hubs.
a. Dependent variable is choice of air carrier and routing for round-trips during 1990.
b. Standard errors are in parentheses. Number of observations is 169; log likelihood at zero is −451.3; log likelihood at convergence is −245.2.
c. The omitted airline dummy variables are for Alaska Airlines and Midway Airlines.

opportunities for the traveler's household. A two-person household could, for instance, find a joint vacation affordable if one person's ticket were free. Thus the marginal value of additional miles to this traveler should be very high. For those travelers who are somewhat farther away from getting a free trip, the effect of additional miles on the value of accumulated miles will be smaller but still noticeable.

On average, the marginal value of additional miles to travelers whose mileage accumulation is neither small nor especially large will be increased because they increase the value of the accumulated miles. The high valuations could also reflect uncertainty discounting: people who do not fly much but fly enough to qualify for a free trip within a reasonable time cannot count on being able to accumulate miles on the carrier of their choice in a predictable manner. If these people are fairly close to qualifying for and anxious to take a free trip, their high valuations of frequent flier miles could reflect their uncertainty as to when they will be able to accumulate additional miles on a particular carrier. Conversely, people who fly a great deal experience little uncertainty as to when they will accumulate miles on a particular carrier, which helps explain why they place a statistically insignificant value on additional miles.

Finally, marketing theory offers a possible explanation for these high valuations. Richard Thaler has argued that consumers derive extra utility from getting something "free."[28] Accordingly, air travelers who are close to receiving a free trip may be willing to pay a much higher fare to obtain the additional miles because of the extra utility they receive.[29]

Turning to the other estimates, we find that on average when someone else pays for their ticket, travelers place a high value, 16.8 cents a mile, on frequent flier mileage. This value is statistically constant across accumulation levels, perhaps because these are people who fly a lot, and the exact point in the cycle of accumulation is not important to them.[30]

28. Richard Thaler, "Mental Accounting and Consumer Choice," *Marketing Science*, vol. 4 (Summer 1985), pp. 199–214. Thaler reported a situation in which people were asked to decide which (or if, in fact, either) person would be more upset: one who sustains $175 in automobile damage or one who sustains $200 in automobile damage but wins $25 in an office pool. Nearly 75 percent of the respondents said the second person is better off; less than 6 percent said neither is better off.

29. Additional perspective on the plausibility of the frequent flier parameter estimates can be obtained by considering average valuations. Because marginal valuations at a specific level of mileage accumulation are not necessarily comparable to an average value over all accumulation levels, we estimated the choice model restricting the four frequent flier mileage coefficients to be equal. The average valuation exceeded 8 cents a mile. In contrast, examples can be constructed that suggest that the average market value of a frequent flier mile could be as high as 4 to 6 cents a mile. To take one case, American Airlines requires 30,000 miles for a free coach trip to Hawaii that normally costs about $1,200, thus yielding a value of 4 cents a mile. (The frequent flier ticket has some blackout restrictions, but no other restrictions such as a Saturday night stay; thus it is more like a coach than a discount ticket.) This figure should then be inflated to include other benefits from frequent flier programs such as special phone reservation numbers and preferred seat selection and boarding pass arrangements. Our finding that travelers' average valuation of frequent flier mileage exceeds the average market valuation can still be explained by the arguments in the text.

30. Using a likelihood ratio test, we did not reject the restriction at the 5 percent level that frequent flier coefficients were the same across different accumulation levels. We also did not reject the restriction at the 5 percent level that the fare and travel time coefficients

The principal-agent problem could also be at work: travelers who do not pay for their tickets may lack incentives to get the lowest fare and shortest travel times; their selection of a carrier may be strongly influenced because they belong to its frequent flier program.[31] In this case the value of frequent flier mileage is about twice as high as the average value travelers place on mileage when they pay for their ticket. This relative valuation is plausible. Finally, air travelers put an inexplicably low value on their time, less than $5.00 an hour.[32] The travel time coefficient, however, is not especially important to this analysis, and the low value could suggest that the fare coefficient, which was used to obtain the high value of frequent flier miles, is not underestimated.

Frequent flier programs are generally thought to provide competitive advantages to large carriers that serve many cities and can offer travelers a variety of destinations when they are entitled to a free trip. This advantage is partly offset, however, by greater air traveler loyalty toward and preference for smaller carriers. The coefficients in table 4-2 indicate that a trip on a smaller carrier increases the likelihood of repeat patronage four times more than a trip on a larger carrier.[33] The smaller carriers are able to set fares nearly $5.00 higher for each accumulated trip than are the larger carriers because of this stronger loyalty.[34] The carrier dummies indicate that, all else equal, travelers prefer two of the smaller carriers, Alaska and Midway, whose dummies are set to zero. These findings are consistent with air traveler surveys, which rank smaller car-

---

were the same for those paying for their own tickets and those whose tickets were purchased by someone else.

31. Frederick J. Stephenson and Richard J. Fox, "Corporate Attitudes toward Frequent-Flier Programs," *Transportation Journal*, vol. 27 (Fall 1987), pp. 10–22, surveyed corporate managers and found that 62 percent of them believed frequent flier programs led to longer travel times because employees chose less convenient flights or less direct routes. Some companies have banded together with a plan to drop frequent flier awards and commissions for travel agents as part of negotiating lower fares with major airlines. See Associated Press, "15 Firms Target Workers' Frequent-Flier Awards," *Washington Post*, June 9, 1994, p. D10.

32. Previous estimates of the value of airline travel time based, for example, on some of the demand studies cited in note 14 exceeded air travelers' average wage.

33. This finding is not as firm as some others because the loyalty coefficient for smaller carriers was not precisely estimated.

34. The "value" of a previous trip on a large carrier is $1.18; the value of a previous trip on a smaller carrier is $6.00. These estimates were obtained as the absolute value of the ratio of the appropriate loyalty coefficient to the fare coefficient. It could be argued that the coefficient for small carrier loyalty represents not so much loyalty as the absence of large carrier alternatives in many markets that the small carriers serve. In our sample, however, small carriers faced competition from larger carriers on 85 percent of their routes.

Table 4-3.   *Estimated Change in Market Share from Elimination of All Frequent Flier Programs, by Airline, 1990*
Percent

Carrier	1990 domestic market share	Change if all carriers eliminate frequent flier programs
American	16.7	−17.8
United	13.2	1.0
Delta	15.8	−0.8
Continental	7.6	−2.7
USAir	15.0	−1.1
Southwest	5.6	10.5
Northwest	8.9	10.3
TWA	5.1	−15.1
Eastern	5.2	12.0
America West	3.9	−2.4
Midway	1.6	23.1
Alaska	1.3	32.4

Source: Authors' calculations using data sources described in the text. Market shares are based on numbers of passengers.

riers higher than larger ones based on their reputation and consumers' favorable travel experiences.[35]

Finally, the statistically insignificant coefficient of the hub dummy shows that a carrier's having a hub at the traveler's place of origin has no effect per se on a traveler's choice of carrier. This does not necessarily mean, however, that the presence of a hub has no effect at all on choice of carrier. It might mean that the effect occurs because a hub leads to other factors, like greater flight frequency, and more frequent fliers.[36]

The results of the carrier choice model were used to investigate the effect of frequent flier programs on market share. Table 4-3 shows the changes in market share from a hypothetical policy that abolishes all frequent flier programs but holds fares, flight frequencies, and other parameters constant. Because fares are increased by frequent flier mileage programs, the changes in market share have probably been over-

35. See, for example, "The Best (and Worst) Airlines," *Consumer Reports*, July 1991, p. 468, satisfaction index based on preflight, in-flight, and postflight service experiences. Alaska and Midway ranked among the top carriers. See also the *Wall Street Journal*, September 15, 1991, where these carriers ranked at the top according to their comfort score.

36. This perspective on hubs was also presented by Alfred E. Kahn, "The Competitive Consequences of Hub Dominance: A Case Study," *Review of Industrial Organization*, vol. 8 (August 1993), pp. 381–405.

stated.[37] Abolishing frequent flier programs would cause larger airlines' fares to fall relative to those of smaller airlines because the larger airlines carry a greater share of passengers redeeming frequent flier miles, which helps curb losses of market share. The choice model was used to predict the market share for each carrier, based on a sample before and after implementation of the policy. The largest carriers would often lose market share from such a policy and the smaller ones would gain.[38] But there are exceptions. As expected, American Airlines, whose frequent flier program is the industry's largest, would be badly hurt, while United Airlines would benefit slightly. American's huge program gives it an advantage over all other carriers. As of 1991 (the end of our survey period), American had 1 million more members in its frequent flier program than its closest competitor, United, and 4 million more than the next closest competitor, Delta.[39] If this advantage were lost, United, with whom American competes in many markets, would gain enough of the market at American's expense to achieve a net benefit.[40] Midway and Alaska would gain significantly from the elimination of the programs, but TWA would lose, apparently because without a frequent flier program it would suffer a serious competitive disadvantage with carriers such as Southwest.

Table 4-4 shows the changes in market share if an individual carrier's frequent flier program were eliminated but other airlines retained their programs. American and United's market shares would fall by more than 50 percent, all else equal.[41] The programs would be less important to Southwest, Midway, and Alaska. The table also shows which carriers compete head-to-head through the programs. If American would lose its program, United and Midway, which like American have Chicago hubs, and Delta, which like American has a Dallas hub, would realize the largest percentage increases in market share.[42] If United would lose its

37. See Morrison and Winston, "Enhancing the Performance of the Deregulated Air Transportation System."

38. These conclusions were not affected when we used the simplified choice model that specified travelers' average valuation of frequent flier miles instead of their marginal valuation at different levels of mileage accumulation.

39. Membership figures were supplied by each carrier.

40. In our sample, American competed with United in 50.7 percent of United's markets, while United competed with American in 44 percent of American's markets.

41. As in the previous simulation, these market share losses are overstated because a carrier's fares are likely to fall if its frequent flier program is eliminated.

42. The conclusions did not change when the changes in market share were measured in percentage points (absolute change) as opposed to percentages (relative change).

Table 4-4. Change in Market Share If One Airlines' Frequent Flier Program Were Eliminated while Other Airlines Maintained Their Programs, 1990
Percent

Carrier	Market share changes of carriers											
	American	United	Delta	Continental	USAir	Southwest	Northwest	TWA	Eastern	America West	Midway	Alaska
American	-53.2	7.4	11.9	2.1	4.7	3.4	0.4	5.0	1.2	1.0	6.5	0
United	32.0	-59.2	10.6	12.9	4.2	0	11.2	15.2	0	3.8	8.8	1.0
Delta	16.4	8.8	-41.8	2.5	0.3	9.0	5.3	3.8	20.3	0.7	0.7	1.0
Continental	1.6	16.4	5.5	-42.8	9.0	6.6	8.3	2.2	4.5	6.2	0	0
USAir	13.3	3.1	5.5	3.7	-25.4	0	2.0	1.1	3.3	1.7	1.2	0
Southwest	1.0	0	1.6	0.7	0	-17.7	0	1.9	0	13.0	0	0
Northwest	0.6	2.8	2.5	6.7	2.3	0	-30.3	4.0	1.8	0	14.3	0
TWA	3.0	5.1	6.2	0.5	0.3	6.8	8.2	-42.3	3.3	0	0.5	0
Eastern	0.3	0.1	5.8	0.3	0.6	0	0.8	0.8	-35.0	0	3.0	0
America West	0	0.1	0.4	1.5	0.1	16.0	0	0	0	-40.7	0	0
Midway	1.0	0.7	0.4	0	0.1	0	2.9	0.4	3.3	0	-17.6	0
Alaska	0	0.2	0	0	0	0	0	0	0	0	0	-2.7

Source: Authors' calculations using data sources described in the text. Market shares are based on numbers of passengers.

program, Continental, Northwest, and TWA as well as American, Delta, and Midway would realize significant market share gains. Smaller and relatively isolated carriers such as Alaska would neither gain market share if other carriers' programs were eliminated nor lose much if their own programs were eliminated.

Travelers obviously differ in the frequency of their trips, their reasons for travel, and the frequency with which someone else pays for their ticket. By offering free trips instead of reduced fares and by using their networks to take advantage of these differences among travelers, large carriers have increased their market share. But smaller carriers can and have offset the competitive advantages of frequent flier programs by charging lower fares and developing stronger customer loyalty. Frequent flier programs are important to competition, but are only one dimension of it. Indeed, they are likely to become less important in the future if carriers increase the number of miles required for free trips, if large corporations can negotiate lower fares in exchange for not participating in the programs, and as miles become easier to obtain without flying— for example, through credit card purchases.[43]

Computer Reservation Systems

As fares and schedules have proliferated under deregulation, travelers' and travel agents' access to information has been facilitated by computer reservation systems (CRS), developed during the mid-1970s by American and United Airlines (table 4-5). Other carriers soon developed their own systems or became partial owners of existing ones. Although the systems were a decided improvement over leafing through paper copies of flight schedules and fares and making many phone calls, they have been criticized for bias in the sense that travel agents are less likely to ticket passengers on carriers other than the host.[44] Such biased information could prevent travelers from getting the lowest available fares or most convenient flights.

43. There have been proposals to tax frequent flier mileage. As discussed in Morrison and Winston, "Enhancing the Performance of the Deregulated Air Transportation System," this would provide revenues to the government, but travelers are not likely to benefit from such a policy because it is not likely to increase airline market entry on a scale that would lower fares by very much.
44. The host of a CRS is the carrier whose internal reservation computer is used by the CRS.

Table 4-5. *Computer Reservation System Ownership*

Computer reservation system	Owners and date ownership began
Apollo	United Airlines (1976)
Galileo International	Covia Partnership of United, USAir, and several foreign partners (1988)
Sabre	American Airlines (1976)
System One	Eastern Airlines (1980), Texas Air Corporation (1983), Continental Airlines (1987)
Pars	TWA (early 1980s), Northwest Airlines (mid-1980s)
Datas II	Delta Airlines (early 1980s)
Worldspan	Partnership of TWA, Northwest, and Delta formed through merger of Pars and Datas II (1990)

Sources: Individual airlines.

Reservation systems can be biased in two ways. In the first type, *display bias*, the host's flights are listed more prominently than those of other carriers, usually at the top of the computer screen. This practice was outlawed by the Civil Aeronautics Board in 1984. The second type, *architectural bias*, often makes it easier for travel agents to obtain information about the host's flights than about others' flights.[45] For example, the system might require fewer keystrokes to get information about the host's flights or might provide more up-to-date information about the host's fares and seat availability. Congress has recently proposed to address this problem by requiring that travel agents be able to book flights for all carriers with equal ease.

To be sure, even a biased CRS can be an improvement over independent search.[46] Besides, a traveler is rarely going to have complete flight information: it is costly to provide everyone with every flight alternative and costly for the traveler to assimilate the information. Still, an architecturally biased system can provide incomplete information, thus narrowing the consumer's choice of carriers. The welfare cost to travelers

45. The term is used in Department of Transportation, "Secretary's Task Force on Competition in the U.S. Domestic Airline Industry: Airline Marketing Practices: Travel Agencies, Frequent-Flier Programs, and Computer Reservation Systems," February 1990.

46. Steven Morrison and Clifford Winston, *The Economic Effects of Airline Deregulation* (Brookings, 1986), provided examples showing that a biased CRS represents an improvement over an independent search if the value of a traveler's search time multiplied by the time spent searching for flight information exceeds the cost of effectively eliminating carrier alternatives because of bias.

depends on the fares and service of the alternatives eliminated. It is, of course, not clear that the costs from CRS bias are attributable to deregulation per se. As the price of computing power dropped, airfares would probably have been computerized and architecturally biased systems developed even if regulation had continued. Nonetheless, the problem of bias has emerged since 1978 and is believed by some to be eroding the benefits from deregulation.

Our carrier choice model from the previous section provides a rough assessment of the possible effects of architectural bias by calculating the loss to travelers from in effect eliminating alternatives.[47] There is, of course, no unambiguous link between architectural bias and the number and types of carriers eliminated. Because sets of carrier choices in the model average three to four carriers, it is reasonable to assume as a base case that at most one carrier alternative—but not always the same carrier—is randomly deleted from a set. However, even if bias is present, travelers do not buy their tickets without asking questions. In particular, they generally choose carriers on which they have frequent flier mileage. Thus, consistent with the carrier choice model, for the base case we did not eliminate a carrier alternative if a traveler pays for his ticket and has accumulated between 3,500 and 80,000 frequent flier miles on that carrier (travelers had a statistically insignificant valuation of additional miles if their accumulations were more than 80,000 or less than 3,500) or if a traveler does not pay for his ticket and has accumulated any frequent flier

---

47. This loss was calculated using the expression for the compensating variation (CV),

$$\frac{-1}{\beta_1}\left[\ln \sum_i \exp (V_i)\right]_{V_1^0}^{V_i^f},$$

where i denotes the travel alternatives, V denotes a traveler's utility, the superscripts for V denote utility before carrier alternatives are eliminated (0) and after carrier alternatives are eliminated (f), and β_1 is a conversion factor equal to the fare coefficient to put the results in monetary units per trip; see Kenneth A. Small and Harvey S. Rosen, "Applied Welfare Economics with Discrete Choice Models," *Econometrica*, vol. 49 (January 1981), pp. 105–30. Aggregate estimates were obtained by calculating the CV as a percentage of the fare for the chosen alternative and multiplying this percentage by industry revenues. Because we did not statistically reject the IIA assumption (see note 24), the estimated coefficients were still consistent when alternatives were deleted or if alternatives were included during estimation when, in fact, they were not considered because of CRS bias. Unfortunately, we did not know whether a particular ticket was booked on a CRS, or the identity of the CRS host if it in fact was booked on a CRS. Thus we may have been overstating the cost of CRS bias because we might have eliminated the CRS host's flight alternative. We did assume that if the chosen carrier did not develop and manage a CRS, no carrier alternatives were eliminated, and thus no welfare change occurred.

Table 4-6.   *Effects of Computer Reservation Systems' Bias on Traveler Welfare and Airline Revenues*
Millions of 1990 dollars

	Assumption[a]		
Effect	Base case	Alternative 1	Alternative 2
Welfare loss: business travelers	138.6	135.9	512.7
Welfare loss: pleasure travelers	295.4	238.4	357.1
Total loss	434.0	374.4	869.7
Revenue transfer to airlines from business travelers	37.7	−10.9	−27.9
Revenue transfer to airlines from pleasure travelers	50.8	43.8	46.6
Total transfer	88.5	32.9	18.7
Deadweight loss	345.5	341.5	851.0

Source: Authors' calculations using data sources described in the text. Totals may not add due to rounding.
a. In all cases, one alternative is randomly eliminated. The assumptions are as follows: Base case: a carrier alternative is not eliminated if a traveler who pays for his ticket has accumulated between 3,500 and 80,000 frequent flier miles on that carrier, or if a traveler who does not pay for his ticket has accumulated any frequent flier miles on that carrier. Alternative 1: a carrier alternative is not eliminated if a traveler who pays for his ticket has accumulated between 3,500 and 80,000 frequent flier miles on that carrier, or if a traveler who does not pay for his ticket has accumulated any frequent flier miles on that carrier, or if that carrier developed and managed its own computer reservation system. Alternative 2: a carrier alternative can be eliminated regardless of whether it has a computer reservation system or whether a traveler has accumulated any frequent flier miles on that carrier. Figures in the table are the average effects from repeated simulations eliminating the type of carrier detailed above.

miles on the carrier. As an alternative to the base case, we also considered a situation in which CRS owners are concerned about retaliation and do not bias their systems against carriers that also manage and own a CRS system. Finally, we considered a worst-case scenario in which any carrier can be eliminated regardless of whether it has a CRS or whether a traveler has accumulated any frequent flier miles on that carrier.

The results of the welfare calculations are shown in table 4-6. In the base case, travelers would lose $434 million (in 1990 dollars) from CRS bias, with people traveling for pleasure losing more than business travelers. Most of the loss, however, would not be in the higher fares that travelers pay because carriers with lower fares are eliminated from consideration. Carriers only gain a net of $89 million from bias, for a deadweight loss—the difference between carrier gains and traveler losses—of $345 million.[48] Surprisingly, the deadweight loss did not result from reduced service (the increases in travel time and decreases in flight frequency were negligible) but from the deletion of carriers with greater

48. Because total trips are held constant in this calculation, to a first approximation total industry costs will not change. Thus the change in total industry revenues is equivalent to the change in industry profit.

Table 4-7. *Effects of Computer Reservation Systems' Bias on
Distribution of Revenue among Airlines, Base Case*
Millions of 1990 dollars

Airline	Revenue change	Airline	Revenue change
American	199.3	TWA	2.6
United	10.8	America West	−12.4
Delta	5.8	Midway	−0.2
Continental	−17.9	Eastern	−29.1
USAir	−46.8	Alaska	0.0
Southwest	−3.4	Total[a]	88.5
Northwest	−20.3		

Source: Authors' calculations using data sources described in the text.
a. Total does not add due to rounding.

brand loyalty and brand preference—the smaller carriers that do not own computer reservations systems).

Travelers' and deadweight losses would fall somewhat if it is assumed that CRS owners are concerned about retaliation and do not allow their systems to eliminate carriers that also manage and own a system (alternative assumption 1). But if, as we have suggested, bias is not strategic, this assumption is unrealistic. Travelers' and deadweight losses increase if any carrier alternative can be eliminated (alternative assumption 2). This indicates that the effects of widespread CRS bias could become a major policy concern, but the assumption is probably an inaccurate characterization of the actual effects of architectural bias. Additional calculations showed that the conclusions were fairly robust to some additional overestimations that assumed that architectural bias causes half the carrier alternatives to be eliminated or causes the carrier alternative with the highest utility to be eliminated.

The redistributive effects of architectural bias for the base case are shown in table 4-7. American Airlines would gain almost $200 million in revenue, but other major CRS owners would gain much less. Carriers without major systems would not lose much revenue.[49]

49. For any given carrier, an increase in revenues will overstate the gain in profits because total costs will also increase from additional passengers. Similarly, a loss in revenue will overstate the profit loss because total costs will decrease with reduced traffic. A separate matter is the booking fees that CRS vendors charge airlines for each flight segment booked by travel agents. According to the Department of Transportation, *Study of Airline Computer Reservation Systems*, DOT-P-37-88-2 (May 1988), in 1986 booking fees averaged $1.14 to $2.07. The ratio of booking fee revenue to cost (including a return on investment) ranged from 65 percent (that is, revenue less than cost) to 276 percent. Using DOT data from *Study of Airline Computer Reservation Systems* and Department of Transportation,

Although the base case is plausible, a closer look at the findings indicates that, if anything, the welfare cost of CRS bias and the effects of redistribution on carriers are significantly overstated because, in fact, many travelers are not passive consumers. The Air Transport Association has reported that 8 percent of air travelers accounted for 44 percent of all air trips in 1993.[50] Most experienced travelers are undoubtedly aware of alternative carriers. And there are strong incentives in the private market to minimize the extent of bias. Corporate travel agencies, many of which agree to be audited, run a serious financial risk if they do not book clients on the least expensive flights. It is therefore not surprising that Topaz Enterprises, the largest auditor of travel agencies, found that from 1989 to mid-1992 nearly 98 percent of the tickets sold by audited agencies were within the travel policy parameters set by their corporate clients.[51] Finally, even occasional fliers will often ask about carriers they prefer. These considerations reinforce our empirical findings that the costs to travelers of architectural bias are small.

The arguments we have advanced are also relevant in assessing the importance of travel agent commission overrides (TACOs), another source of possible anticompetitive behavior in which airlines pay travel agents additional commissions if the agents meet certain volume or market share targets. It is difficult, however, to develop a base-case (and as we argue in the CRS analysis, a worst-case) empirical analysis illustrating that TACOs have little effect on traveler behavior because commission override information is confidential. Nonetheless, the General Accounting Office concluded that the anticompetitive effect of TACOs has probably been less important than the effects of frequent flier programs and computer reservation systems.[52] TACOs' influence on travel by large corporations is also probably insignificant because of the increased use of auditing. Finally, the expected growth of travel kiosks, where travelers can obtain airline tickets by, for example, purchasing them at supermarkets, and the possible widespread adoption of ticketless travel is

"Secretary's Task Force on Competition," in 1988 these markups resulted in a transfer from non-CRS owner airlines to CRS owners of $262 million.

50. The Gallup Organization, *Air Travel Survey* (1993), produced for the Air Transport Association, Washington. In 1992, 8 percent of travelers accounted for 46 percent of trips; 7 percent accounted for 40 percent of trips in 1991.

51. Personal communication from Jeanie M. Thompson-Smith, President, Topaz Enterprises, Inc.

52. General Accounting Office, *Airline Competition*.

likely to reduce the number of travel agencies and commission override practices.[53]

Patterns of Price Leadership

Thus far we have analyzed the effects on travelers' welfare of various marketing and operating strategies by individual airlines. We now turn to behavior that is jointly undertaken by two or more airlines. Of particular interest is a practice called price leadership, in which an airline proposes a fare change, sees if other airlines follow its lead, and then reacts accordingly. Price leadership is harmful to travelers if carriers are able to raise fares above what they would have been if they had been set independently. This practice has become a concern since deregulation because the smaller number of effective competitors at the national level makes it more likely that they will cooperate on fares and less likely that an independent carrier will disrupt the agreement by charging lower fares. Price leadership may also have been facilitated by a centralized computerized airfare database (maintained by Airline Tariff Publishers) to the extent that this database enables carriers to test the waters about other carriers' reactions to possible fare changes. The Department of Justice has investigated collusion among carriers on fare increases.[54] In 1994 several airlines signed a consent decree not to post ending dates for their fare filings. Following the settlement, the Justice Department estimated that such price signaling had cost travelers $2 billion a year.[55]

Here we have provided circumstantial empirical evidence as to how price leadership might work and what its costs could be to travelers. First, we used a methodology called Granger causality to test whether knowledge of, for example, American's fares in a given period improves the accuracy of forecasts of United's fares in later periods.[56] If so, American's fares are said to cause United's fares. The difficulty with causality find-

---

53. For a discussion of the various ways that ticketless travel is being introduced by airlines, for example, providing frequent travelers with computer-chip encoded cards that are scanned by a gate agent, see Perry Flint, "The Electronic Skyway," *Air Transport World*, vol. 32 (January 1995), p. 38.

54. See, for example, Asra Q. Nomani, "U.S. Probes Whether Airlines Colluded on Fare Increase," *Wall Street Journal*, December 14, 1989, sec. 2, p. 1.

55. See Joe Davidson, "Six Big Airlines Settle U.S. Suit on Price Fixing," *Wall Street Journal*, March 18, 1994, p. A2.

56. For more details of time series econometrics and causality tests see, for example, A. C. Harvey, *The Econometric Analysis of Time Series*, 2d ed. (Philip Allan, 1990).

ings is that by themselves they are purely descriptive. Moreover, in this application the coinciding movement of fares could be consistent with perfect competition as well as with price leadership. So the fact that airline fares rise and fall together tells little about whether there is price leadership. To overcome this problem, we subjected our findings to additional empirical analyses, which included estimating models and performing calculations that lent credence to the conclusion that the causality patterns were consistent with price leadership and at variance with perfect competition. In the final step we estimated the cost of this behavior to travelers.[57]

The causality test assesses whether the current fares of airline i can be predicted by the past fares of airline j, where the past fares could be one, or two, or more periods in the past. To make the statistical argument convincing, there are two additional safeguards. One is that confidence in the finding of causality increases if several different lags show the same result. The other includes in the test past fares for airline i, to make sure that the result is due to the fares for the other airline and not just a matter of saying that fares in the past help to explain fares in the present.[58]

---

57. To be sure, there are theories of collusion and explanations of noncollusion for coinciding movements of prices that causality analysis does not account for, but these are either not especially relevant for airlines or we were able to assess them by extending our analysis. For example, a literature has developed that has attempted to detect tacit collusion by testing whether alternative repeated game strategies are consistent with actual pricing behavior during price wars; see, for example, Margaret E. Slade, "Vancouver's Gasoline-Price Wars: An Empirical Exercise in Uncovering Supergame Strategies," *Review of Economic Studies*, vol. 59 (April 1992), pp. 257–76. This approach appears to be difficult to apply to the airline industry because multiple prices, markets, and carriers require strongly maintained assumptions to enable estimation of reaction functions to be tractable. It is also not clear what theoretical repeated game strategies could apply to this industry, especially because the most prominent ones in practice appear to involve cross-market interactions (for example, a carrier responds to price changes by a rival airline in one market by changing its price in another market where it competes with that airline). It is possible that causality could falsely attribute correlated price movements to price leadership when in fact they are the result of either common cost influences or past demand shocks. We later distinguish between those explanations and price leadership by determining whether findings of causality are associated with higher price-cost margins on airline routes.

58. Statistically, subject to certain technical conditions, the causality test amounts to estimating fare regressions of the form

$$Fare_{i,t} = \alpha + \beta_1 Fare_{i,t-1} + \cdots + \beta_n Fare_{i,t-n} + \gamma_1 Fare_{j,t-1} + \cdots + \gamma_n Fare_{j,t-n},$$

where subscripts i and j refer to airlines and the t subscripts refer to time periods. If we can reject the null hypothesis that $\gamma_1 = \gamma_2 = \cdots = \gamma_n = 0$, airline j's fares are said to cause airline i's fares. Although the number of lagged variables to include is arbitrary, we have more confidence in a finding of causality when it is found for more than one lag. The

We carried out causality tests on competitive pairs of carriers that had flown the same route for several years. The sample was constructed using the 1,000 most heavily traveled domestic origin-destination routes, accounting for two-thirds of all domestic passenger trips in 1990. We assembled quarterly data for each route from the fourth quarter of 1978 until the fourth quarter of 1991. Of the 1,000 routes, 400 had two or more carriers that had competed with each other for at least twenty consecutive quarters, and had valid data involving 817 competitive pairs.[59] The null hypothesis was that causality was not present. Our base case used the average fare, a 10 percent significance level, and a lag of one quarter.[60] Additional tests presented in the appendix to this chapter used alternative assumptions, but they did not alter the conclusions reached in the base case. The fare series that satisfied the causality test conditions generated a final sample of 806 causality tests covering 245 routes (see the appendix).

The results of the causality tests are summarized in table 4-8. The rows show the percentage of a carrier's causality tests in which its fares cause another carrier's fares (for instance, American's fares cause another carrier's fares in 39 percent of American's competitive pairs). The columns show the percentage of a carrier's causality tests in which its

---

technical conditions under which a causality test can be carried out are detailed in the appendix to this chapter. In brief, to test causality between two fare series, both series must be stationary, which means that the mean and variance of the series are finite and independent of time and that the covariance between two observations must only depend on the time difference between the two observations. Stationarity is tested statistically using an augmented Dickey-Fuller test (see Harvey, *Econometric Analysis of Time Series*).

59. The source of our fare data was the Department of Transportation's Origin-Destination Survey (Data Bank 1A). Because fares may change more frequently than each quarter, it may have been preferable to have daily fare data. Unfortunately, the only available data are quarterly. The implications of using aggregated data for our analysis are not clear. We selected twenty quarters as the time period that would generate a minimum number of observations to conduct the causality test. We did not consider quarters for which a carrier had fewer than 100 sampled direct passengers on a route, which amounts to about 75 passengers a week. Our sample included one-way tickets with one destination (no connecting flights or intermediate stops) and round-trip tickets with one destination (passenger returns to origin after flight to destination). We excluded trips with more than one coupon in each direction to be sure that the fare paid was for a particular origin-destination itinerary. Given the nature of the information in Data Bank 1A, it is impossible to tell if an intermediate city on a routing represents a connection or an additional destination.

60. We used a fare screen to eliminate possible coding errors in the fare variable. If fares were unreasonably high or low (using the General Accounting Office's fare screen), they were eliminated from the sample. This procedure eliminated frequent flier fares, which was appropriate because we were interested in testing causality of fares actually charged.

Table 4-8. *Share of Airline Competitive Pairs in Which One Airline Has Caused Another's Fare (Causality), Base Case with Average Fare, 10 Percent Significance Level, One Lag, 1978–91*
Percent

Carrier causing fares	Carrier's fare being caused										
	American	Continental	Delta	Eastern	Northwest	Pan American	TWA	United	USAir	Others	Total
American	...	14.3	48.1	...	66.7	25.0	60.0	30.8	33.3	33.3	39.2
Continental	42.9	...	0	0	25.0	0	...	11.1	0	0	13.5
Delta	18.5	50.0	...	19.6	66.7	0	22.2	22.2	0	33.3	22.7
Eastern	...	50.0	39.1	...	20.0	33.3	0	0	0	8.3	28.2
Northwest	50.0	33.3	16.7	0	...	0	33.3	26.7	25.0	0	18.3
Pan American	0	0	0	33.3	0	...	28.6	33.3	0	0	15.4
TWA	10.0	...	25.0	0	66.7	28.6	...	11.8	0	50.0	22.6
United	20.0	22.2	44.4	40.0	33.3	0	29.4	...	50.0	21.4	25.3
USAir	0	0	0	33.3	75.0	0	40.0	50.0	...	0	25.9
Others[a]	50.0	0	0	25.0	37.5	0	0	32.1	...	15.4	20.3
Total	22.3	19.6	35.2	20.5	42.6	15.4	28.6	23.4	11.1	16.7	24.3

Source: Authors' calculations based on data sources described in the text.
a. Others are Aloha, Alaska, Frontier, Hawaiian, America West, TranStar, Midway, New York, Air California, Ozark, People Express, Piedmont, Pacific Southwest, Republic, Britt, Western, Southwest. Although separate causality tests were run for each carrier in this category, the results are presented together for simplicity.

fares are caused by another carrier's fares (American's fares are caused by another carrier's fares in 22 percent of American's competitive pairs). American clearly emerges as the industry fare leader; United appears relatively passive.[61] Continental and Northwest have somewhat low causality percentages except against each other and American. Notwithstanding American's influence, the presence of fare causality throughout the industry occurs in only 24 percent of the tests.

These results help explain the optimism behind and the subsequent failure of American's attempt in the early 1990s to stabilize airfares by convincing other carriers to adopt its pricing regimen. In April 1992 American introduced a value-pricing initiative that simplified existing fare structures by offering four basic fares and slashed full-fare coach and first-class fares. Given that American's fares cause other carriers' fares on a fairly high percentage of the routes on which they compete, the airline's optimism that the industry would adopt the value-pricing strategy was understandable. What American apparently did not realize, however, was that causality occurs far less often in markets that it does not serve. If American's pricing strategy were to be followed by another carrier, that carrier would be expected to adopt this strategy throughout its network. American's influence turned out to be too limited to get other carriers to follow its lead, especially in markets where they did not compete with American. By October 1992 Robert L. Crandall, chairman of American, had abandoned value pricing: "We tried to provide some price leadership but it didn't work, so we are back into the death by a thousand cuts."[62]

This anecdotal evidence is consistent with an interpretation that our causality tests showed some form of price leadership. To develop some circumstantial empirical evidence, we began by investigating whether causality occurred on particular types of routes. One way of tackling this

61. Some industry analysts have pointed out that Southwest Airlines is the low-cost fare leader in many of its markets. We could not confirm this because there were not enough competitive pairs in our sample involving Southwest that covered a sufficient length of time. In any event, spanning fourteen years, our causality tests would only have picked up behavior that was of relatively long duration. Southwest's ascendancy is somewhat recent.

62. Coleman Lollar, "Back to the Bad Old Days," *Frequent Flyer*, December 1992, p. 8. To be sure, other factors were important. TWA probably viewed American's cuts in full-fare coach and first-class fares as directed toward them and the special fares they offered through St. Louis to attract business travel. At the same time, Northwest may have been trying to generate cash with a 50-percent-off sale and subsequently triggered the 1992 fare war. Other carriers believed American's new fares were predatory, but Continental and Northwest failed to prove this in court.

Table 4-9.   *Extent of Causality Airlines Have at Their Hubs and
Overall, by Airport, 1978–91*
Percent

Airport	Causality tests for all carriers at airport	Causality tests for hub carrier[a]
Atlanta	28	Delta 18 (23), Eastern 44 (28)
Boston	26	No dominant hub carriers
Charlotte	40	Piedmont 50 (45)
Chicago O'Hare	29	American 34 (39), United 30 (25)
Dallas–Ft. Worth	33	American 46 (39), Delta 22 (23)
Denver	21	Frontier 38 (38), United 17 (25)
Detroit	22	Northwest 22 (18)
Houston	25	Continental 14 (14)
Las Vegas	25	No dominant hub carriers
Los Angeles	23	No dominant hub carriers
Miami	28	Eastern 30 (28)
Minneapolis	52	Northwest 50 (18), Republic 0 (8)
Newark	35	Continental 0 (14)
New York Kennedy	11	Pan Am 10 (15), TWA 13 (23)
New York LaGuardia	19	No dominant hub carriers
Orlando	7	No dominant hub carriers
Phoenix	11	America West 0 (0), Southwest 0 (15)
Pittsburgh	21	USAir 17 (26)
San Francisco	23	United 23 (25)
St. Louis	30	Ozark 13 (9), TWA 38 (23)

Source: Authors' calculations based on data described in the text.
a. Hub carrier's causality percentage for all airports is in parentheses.

question was to examine the extent of causality that an airline had at its
hubs (table 4-9) and compare the results with the amount of an airline's
overall causality (reproducing data in table 4-8). Although this test would
seem a straightforward enough way of finding out whether airlines have
more power at their own hubs, the results were mixed. The percentage
of Delta's tests showing causality on routes involving Atlanta was less
than Delta's causality average. The same is true for United at Denver,
USAir at Pittsburgh, and others. But the percentage of Eastern's tests
showing causality on routes involving Atlanta was higher than Eastern's
causality average. This was also the case for Northwest at Minneapolis,
TWA at St. Louis, and others. Given that the presence of fare causality
over all routes was 24 percent, the presence of fare causality does not
appear, in general, to be significantly greater for routes that have a hub
airport at the origin or destination.

Because this rough attempt to provide an economic interpretation of the causality findings—their connection to competition at an airport— seemed to lack power to reach a conclusion, we employed a more formal set of statistical tools. We estimated a probit regression to analyze whether the presence of causality could be explained by the amount of competition on a route and other route characteristics. If what we were observing was in fact some form of price leadership, the presence of causality should have been inversely related to the amount of competition on the route. If coinciding movements in prices were a reflection of competition, however, the presence of causality should have been directly related to the amount of competition on the route. (In the limiting case of perfect competition, an additional competitor should have no effect on the presence of causality because prices would already move together.) The dependent variable for the base case was defined as one if the competitive pair exhibited causality (with one lag) and zero if it did not.[63] The explanatory variables paralleled those used in the baseline fare equation described in chapter 3. We measured competition by the number of effective competitors on the route (route competition) and the minimum number of effective competitors at each end of the route (airport competition).[64] We also included distance and a measure of traffic density equal to the number of direct passengers traveling between the route's origin and destination (route passengers). Finally, we extended the specification by adding a set of dummy variables indicating the carrier and direction of causality being tested ("causing" or "being caused"). These variables were included to capture unmeasured carrier-specific influences on causality such as carrier reputation and historical leader-follower relationships.

63. An alternative to the 0-1 dichotomous dependent variable that we used would have been to use a continuous variable equal to the significance level of the test for causality— that is, how certain were we that causality existed? However, because the conclusions we reached were generally robust using different critical significance levels to define the presence of causality, our choice of dependent variable should not have affected our conclusions. To distinguish those carriers whose presence on a route leads to causality because they are more likely to cause another carrier's fares from those carriers whose presence leads to causality because they are more likely to have their fares caused by another carrier, each competitive pair contributed four observations to the regression (A causing B, A getting caused by B, B causing A, B getting caused by A).

64. The number of effective competitors is the inverse of the Herfindahl index as defined in chapter 2. Route competition is based on market shares of each carrier on a route, and airport competition is based on the share of total enplanements at each airport on a route.

Table 4-10.   *Probit Analysis of Factors Affecting Causality, by Airline*[a]

Variable	Coefficient estimate	Standard error	t-value	Prob > |t|
Constant	−0.34694	0.0240	−14.46	0.000
American: being caused	0.09699	0.0274	3.54	0.000
American: causing	0.63541	0.0259	24.54	0.000
Continental: being caused	0.06721	0.0378	1.78	0.075
Continental: causing	−0.15592	0.0401	−3.88	0.000
Delta: being caused	0.49228	0.0254	19.35	0.000
Delta: causing	0.05801	0.0267	2.18	0.030
Eastern: being caused	0.03432	0.0309	1.11	0.267
Eastern: causing	0.32786	0.0295	11.12	0.000
Northwest: being caused	0.81411	0.0318	25.60	0.000
Northwest: causing	0.16665	0.0349	4.77	0.000
Pan American: being caused	0.05698	0.0482	1.18	0.237
Pan American: causing	0.04117	0.0485	0.85	0.396
TWA: being caused	0.44432	0.0318	13.99	0.000
TWA: causing	0.21937	0.0332	6.61	0.000
United: being caused	0.19966	0.0246	8.11	0.000
United: causing	0.28447	0.0244	11.67	0.000
USAir: being caused	−0.29258	0.0555	−5.27	0.000
USAir: causing	0.23604	0.0469	5.03	0.000
Distance	−2.327E-5	8.528E-6	−2.73	0.006
Route competition	−0.10334	0.0064	−16.23	0.000
Airport competition	−0.08671	0.0039	−22.29	0.000
Route passengers	9.658E-6	6.501E-7	14.86	0.000

Source: Authors' calculations based on data sources described in the text.
a. Dependent variable is cause (1 if competitive pair exhibits Granger causality, 0 if it does not). Number of observations = 60,148; log likelihood for full model = −32,558.4; log likelihoood for restricted model = −34,000.1.

The results are what would be expected if causality is reflecting some form of price leadership.[65] Its presence is less likely when competition at the route level and at the airport level increases, but is more likely when traffic density increases (table 4-10). Paralleling previous findings concerning conditions that facilitate noncompetitive behavior, fewer competitors are more conducive to price leadership.[66] But, holding competition

65. Because we used the full data set from the causality tests, which included each carrier and the direction of causality being tested, the observations may not be completely independent (that is, error terms for a given carrier whose causality is tested in both directions may be correlated). We found, however, that our conclusions and their statistical reliability were not particularly affected when we used subsets of the full data set that, for example, included observations based on tests of just one direction of causality.
66. See, in a different context, George J. Stigler, "A Theory of Oligopoly," *Journal of Political Economy*, vol. 72 (February 1964), pp. 44–61.

constant, a larger market increases the rewards from price leadership.[67] The estimates are also consistent with the initial finding that there is a variation in the extent to which each carrier's fares cause or are caused by other carriers' fares.[68] The dummy variables that reflect this indicate, as in table 4-8, that the greatest likelihood of causality occurs when American is causing another carrier's fares and when Northwest's fares are being caused. Finally, the presence of causality decreases with route length, perhaps because we analyzed fares on direct routes. Pricing on long-haul direct routes may be influenced by the fares of competing connecting routes rather than simply by competing direct flights.

Fare causality is present in about one-fourth of the causality tests and present on routes in a systematic way consistent with some sort of price leadership. Since the causality findings appeared to be reflecting a potentially important economic phenomenon, rather than being a statistical artifact, it seemed useful to estimate their implications for travelers' welfare. We did this by estimating and comparing price-cost margins on routes with and without causality. The methodology for estimating route-specific costs, which are needed to calculate the margins, is described in the appendix to this chapter. Given these costs, we used the average fare for each route to form price-cost margins. Under our base-case assumptions the price-cost margin was 6.2 percentage points higher on routes with causality than on those without causality, and this difference was statistically significant.[69]

67. These findings were generally robust using different definitions of causality (significance level and lag length) and for logs as well as levels.

68. We were able to reject the null hypothesis that the coefficients of the dummy variables were equal at the 1 percent significance level, indicating that carrier identity does matter.

69. This was tested using a randomized test. In a randomized test the distribution of the test statistic under the null hypothesis is generated iteratively by computer through repeated shuffling of the data. The null hypothesis was that causality and price-cost margins were unrelated. The significance level of the test was calculated by shuffling the data so that no relationship exists between causality and price-cost margins. First the price-cost margin was calculated for all causality tests. Then the difference between those that exhibited causality and those that did not was calculated, showing that airlines in a competitive pair with causality had a price-cost margin 6.2 percentage points higher than when causality was not found. Next the price-cost margin data were shuffled relative to the presence or absence of causality so that the two were indeed independent. The difference between price-cost margins for those tests in which causality was present (because of shuffling) and those where it was not was calculated. Through repeated shuffling (10,000 times in this case) the percentage of the time that the calculated difference under the null hypothesis exceeded the observed difference (without shuffling) was the significance level of the

This finding could, of course, be biased because of differences between routes with and without causality. It may be, for example, that fares are higher on routes that show causality, not because one airline is offering price leadership but because some other factors are leading both to the finding of causality and to the higher fares. We therefore used the baseline fare equation from chapter 3, which already controlled for route distance, the extent of route and airport competition, and a measure of traffic density, to control for carrier-specific effects, specifying dummy variables that indicated which carrier's fares were being explained (all the continuous variables were measured as they were before and were in natural logarithms).[70] To estimate the effect of causality on fares we added a causation dummy ("cause") equal to one when the causality test was positive and zero otherwise.[71] We tested whether the coefficients of the carrier dummies were the same and were able to reject that hypothesis at the 1 percent significance level (table 4-11). As expected, fares increase with distance, but less than proportionately. They decrease as route competition, airport competition, and route density increase. Finally, routes for which causation is present have fares 4.8 percent higher than noncausal routes, all else equal.[72] This estimate is consistent with the estimate obtained from the simple price-cost margin calculations. If we were, in fact, capturing the effects of perfect competition, there would have been no economic or statistical difference between the fare-cost margins on routes with causality and on those without, and the causation dummy in the fare equation would have been economically and statisti-

---

test. In our case, after 10,000 shuffles only 0.01 percent were larger than the observed difference. See Eric W. Noreen, *Computer-Intensive Methods for Testing Hypotheses: An Introduction* (John Wiley, 1989).

70. The specification omitted carrier dummies for the smaller ("other") carriers (Aloha, Alaska, and so on); thus these other carriers were the normalized or base effect.

71. Analogous to the probit regression, each carrier's fare in any time period and competitive pair entered the regression twice, once for observations involving whether they caused their paired carrier's fares and once for observations involving whether their fares were caused by their paired carrier's fares. As before, the conclusions were not affected by using smaller data sets that included data based on causality tests in one direction.

72. To explore endogeneity concerns, we instrumented cause, using the probit equation and variants of it, and found little change in the estimated parameters. As we noted in chapter 3, there has been an unresolved debate about the appropriateness of treating competition measures as exogenous in fare regressions. However, our primary interest in the fare regression was to use the causality variable to corroborate the price-cost margin estimate. The exogeneity debate should therefore not detract from the consistent findings of our two approaches.

Table 4-11. *Factors Influencing Fares*[a]

Variable	Coefficient estimate	Heteroskedastic-consistent standard error	t-value	Prob > |t|
Constant	2.156	0.016	135.403	0.000
American	0.292	0.006	52.487	0.000
Continental	0.165	0.007	23.685	0.000
Delta	0.239	0.005	46.083	0.000
Eastern	0.186	0.005	36.421	0.000
Northwest	0.189	0.005	34.632	0.000
Pan American	0.042	0.007	5.908	0.000
TWA	0.147	0.006	23.733	0.000
United	0.257	0.005	52.614	0.000
USAir	0.229	0.007	31.791	0.000
Ln(distance)	0.526	0.002	334.220	0.000
Ln(route competition)	− 0.121	0.004	− 29.345	0.000
Ln(airport competition)	− 0.047	0.003	− 14.952	0.000
Ln(route passengers)	− 0.113	0.002	− 75.104	0.000
Cause	0.048	0.003	16.698	0.000

Source: Authors' calculations based on data sources described in the text.
a. Dependent variable is ln (real fare). Number of observations = 60,148; R^2 = 0.720.

cally insignificant. Thus both estimates reinforce the previous finding that what we were measuring is the effect of some form of price leadership.

How important is this to travelers? The fare increases due to causality amount to between 0.6 percent (based on the fare regression) and 0.9 percent (based on the price-cost margin) of domestic passenger revenues for the entire sample, resulting in a total annual cost to travelers for all domestic routes of $365 million in 1993 dollars.[73] These costs partially overlap with fare premiums from hubs because some causality exists on routes with hub airports. Thus to the extent that fare causality indicates the presence of price leadership, the cost to travelers has been small. In particular, it is a very small fraction of the $12 billion annual benefit to them from lower deregulated fares and much below the Justice Depart-

73. These percentage figures are lower than the respective regression and price-cost margin effects because they include all routes, that is, routes with and without causality, routes that could not have causality (one-carrier routes), and routes that we did not test because of too few observations. The welfare cost to travelers was obtained by multiplying the airline industry's 1993 domestic passenger revenue, $48.7 billion as reported by the Air Transport Association, by 0.75 percent, the average of our two estimates of fare elevation. (This simple procedure overstates the welfare cost of any given fare increase because it assumes that all travelers continue to fly at the higher fare.) The cost to travelers is even lower when we raised the significance levels of the causality tests, with the lowest cost equal to $85 million when a 1 percent significance level is used.

ment's estimated $2 billion annual cost from price signaling by major airlines.[74]

The Welfare Cost of Fare Restrictions

Carrier practices, individually or collectively, affect travelers' welfare through the fares they pay and the quality of the service they receive. Since deregulation, airlines have significantly increased their practice of sorting passengers and charging them different fares according to their ability to meet certain travel restrictions. For example, carriers have attached advance purchase and reservation requirements and a Saturday night stay to their discount fares. As they always have, travelers self-select into appropriate fare categories. The few who cannot or will not meet any restrictions fly at unrestricted full fares; the vast majority who can meet some or all restrictions choose from a range of discount fares.

The resulting proliferation of fares has enabled an increasing number of fliers to travel at some discount from full coach fares.[75] But the restrictions exact costs, primarily in the form of less convenient service, and the costs must be taken into account in evaluations of the effect of deregulation on travelers. It would be misleading, for example, simply to compare a $600 full-fare unrestricted ticket purchased under CAB regulation with a $300 discount ticket with many travel restrictions that was purchased since deregulation.

Restrictions would not exact welfare costs directly if airlines were able to classify consumers without increasing their travel costs. Travelers who intend to stay a Saturday night, for example, would not bear additional welfare costs because their travel plans call for this stay. Inconvenienced travelers might choose an unrestricted fare rather than extend their trip until Sunday (then the only welfare cost would be if prices were above marginal cost). Because travelers do not fall into neat boxes, however, restrictions are likely to increase costs for some in the form of inconvenience.

Three factors determine the costs of restrictions: the actual restrictions, the traveler characteristics that determine how they are affected by restrictions, and the extent to which travelers adapt their behavior in

74. Davidson, "Six Big Airlines Settle U.S. Suit."
75. According to the Air Transport Association, 37 percent of all travelers flew at a discounted fare under regulation in 1977. This figure has more than doubled during deregulation.

response to fare differentials. We estimated these costs using a binary logit model of travelers' choice of restricted or unrestricted air travel. The decision to travel was taken as given.[76] The travel restrictions we included were advance reservation requirements, required Saturday night stay, cancellation penalty, and advance purchase requirements.[77] Because the effect of the restrictions would likely depend on whether a traveler could plan ahead and easily extend his trip beyond Saturday, we interacted the restrictions with the purpose of the traveler's trip (business or pleasure).[78] The model was estimated based on a survey of 220 air travelers conducted in May and November 1990.[79]

Initial estimations showed that the restrictions imposed no statistically significant costs on pleasure travelers, presumably because they have little difficulty planning trips in advance that extend through a weekend.[80] But

76. This assumption was innocuous for our purposes because we were interested in estimating the inconvenience costs of restrictions to people who do travel in order to make a proper adjustment to our previous estimate of the effects of fare deregulation. If restrictions were outlawed, fewer people would be likely to travel because average fares would probably rise. This is especially true because a major benefit to all travelers from carriers' being able to set restricted discount fares is that discounted fares help fill up planes, which lowers average costs and keeps average fares lower. Thus because travel restrictions enable more people to fly, the attendant service quality costs are probably overstated in our framework, which does not give people the option to cancel their travel. However, as indicated earlier, these extra costs were irrelevant to our primary purpose.

77. We also included other restrictions such as specific days on which travel could occur, but this effect was insignificant. The general effect of a minimum stay requirement and restricted days of travel was captured in the Saturday night stay. We also explored different functional specifications of the restrictions and different interaction variables concerning how far in advance discount tickets had to be purchased and what reservation restrictions applied. These explorations did not lead to any material changes in the reported findings.

78. We also interacted the restrictions with other trip purposes such as attending a funeral and mixed (business and pleasure) activities, but these additional interactions did not produce any statistically significant effects. Initial specifications also included household income and trip distance to account for the effect these variables have on load factor, but these variables were insignificant.

79. The sample was based on a diary survey conducted by Allison-Fisher, Inc. Respondents were asked in advance to keep records of their air travel and report both restricted and unrestricted travel alternatives and their choice. As in the carrier choice analysis, the sample contained more than one trip by the same traveler in a few instances, but estimation of models using only one random trip from each traveler produced results that were very close to the models in which repeat observations were included.

80. Because our data included only one restricted alternative, we were not able to analyze choices of which restricted fare travelers pick from an array of possibilities. Including additional restricted alternatives might reveal costs to pleasure travelers from restrictions.

Table 4-12. *Factors Influencing Traveler Choice of Airline Ticket*[a]

Variable	Business travelers coefficient[b]
Fare (dollars)	−0.0087
	(0.0023)
Advance reservation requirement (days)	−0.0320
	(0.0268)
Saturday night stay (1 if required, 0 otherwise)	−1.902
	(0.711)
Cancellation penalty for fares with 21-day advance purchase requirement (percent of fare)	−0.0027
	(0.0121)

Source: Authors' calculations based on data sources described in the text.
a. Dependent variable is choice of restricted or unrestricted fare. Number of observations = 80; log likelihood at zero = −55; log likelihood at convergence = −42.
b. Standard errors are in parentheses.

business travelers did incur statistically significant costs from at least some of the restrictions (table 4-12). The Saturday night restriction was particularly onerous; the typical business traveler attached a $219 disutility to it. (This figure was obtained as the ratio of the coefficient for Saturday night stay to the fare coefficient. It can be interpreted as an additional cost of delaying the return trip.) Because this restriction forces some business travelers to spend an extra day in a possibly unfamiliar city instead of spending leisure time at home with family or friends, this magnitude is plausible.[81] Advance reservation requirements imposed a cost estimated at $3.68 a day (the ratio of the coefficient for the advance reservation requirement to the fare coefficient), but its statistical significance was not high. The cancellation penalty had a statistically insignificant cost.[82]

We estimated the costs of the restrictions to business travelers by calculating the amount of money they could sacrifice if the restrictions were lifted and be as well off as they were when the restrictions were in place.[83] The compensating variation from eliminating the restrictions

81. The cost of the Saturday night restriction was not found to be affected by who paid for the travel.
82. The cancellation penalty, measured as a percentage of fare, included the extreme case of no refund, in which case the variable equaled 100.
83. As stated previously, the expression for the compensating variation (CV) that we calculated is

$$\frac{-1}{\beta_1}\left[\ln \sum_i \exp\left(\beta X_i\right)\right]_{\beta X_i^0}^{\beta X_i^1},$$

where β denotes the set of coefficient estimates from the fare choice model, X denotes the amounted to $87 for each business trip, with $67 of the benefits gained by eliminating the Saturday night stay.[84] Although costly, the restrictions were worth bearing for many travelers because the average differential between restricted and unrestricted fares in the sample was $220.

The aggregate annual cost of the restrictions to business travelers is $5 billion in 1990 dollars. This estimate was obtained by multiplying the cost per business trip ($87) by the number of business trips taken by air in 1990 (57.6 million, estimated by the U.S. Travel Center in Washington).[85] Although the $5 billion offsets to some extent the benefits to travelers from obtaining a discount fare, it is not the appropriate figure to adjust the benefits from deregulation. Restrictions also existed during regulation, and business travelers suffered costs from them. After estimating the proportion of business travelers who suffered inconvenience costs from travel restrictions under regulation, we concluded that the benefits from lower deregulated fares estimated previously—$12.4 billion annually in 1993 dollars—should be reduced by $1.1 billion to account for the cost of restrictions attached to discounted travel (see the appendix to this chapter). This important adjustment still leaves travelers $11.3 billion better off from fare deregulation.

---

set of explanatory variables, i denotes the fare alternatives, the superscripts for X denote the value of the variables before the restrictions are eliminated (0) and after the restrictions are eliminated (1), and β_1 is a conversion factor equal to the fare coefficient to put the results in monetary units per business trip.

The CV measures benefits to business travelers from improvements in their chosen alternative after the policy change (that is, travelers who choose restricted travel benefit from elimination of the restrictions) and measures benefits to travelers who switch to an alternative that is now preferred after the policy change (unrestricted travelers, for example, may benefit by switching to lower restricted fares with the restrictions eliminated). Because we were interested in the cost of restrictions to those who actually incur them, the CV was calculated with the constraint that travelers who selected the unrestricted alternative were unable to switch to the restricted alternative after the restrictions are eliminated.

84. This figure is less than the disutility attached to the Saturday night restriction in the fare choice model because the Saturday night figure reflects the costs to those travelers who actually incur this restriction, that is, those who dislike a Saturday night stay do not choose to stay. The cost from the other components was $25.27 for advance reservations and $1.60 for the cancellation penalty. The sum of the components is not equal to the total welfare change because the CV measure is nonlinear.

85. Because most of these costs are based on the highly statistically significant fare and Saturday night stay coefficients, the estimate should be reliable. A recent complication is that some travelers are apparently buying several restricted tickets and using them for parts of a trip to avoid the restrictions. The total fare from buying multiple restricted tickets is lower than the unrestricted fare. Our sample did not capture this phenomenon; thus we could be overstating the aggregate cost of the restrictions.

Table 4-13. *Annual Gains to Travelers from Airline Deregulation*
Billions of 1993 dollars

Category	Gain	Category	Gain
Fares	12.4[a]	Mix of connections (on-line or interline)	0.9[f]
Travel restrictions	−1.1[b]		
Frequency	10.3[c]	Travel time	−2.8[g]
Load factor	−0.6[d]	Total	18.4
Number of connections	−0.7[e]		

Source: Authors' calculations. See text for details.
a. See p. 13.
b. See p. 81.
c. See p. 21.
d. See p. 25.
e. See p. 35.
f. See p. 35.
g. See p. 24.

Of course, the question remains whether carriers will further tighten restrictions and impose greater welfare costs, but this seems unlikely because the most costly restriction—the Saturday night stay—segments the market reasonably well. Additional restrictions such as two Saturday night stays are not likely to segment it any better. And recent changes, such as more flexible itinerary changes for trips on tickets with restricted fares, indicate a movement toward somewhat less onerous restrictions.

Summary

The occasional traveler, confronting complex travel restrictions for some discount fares, hearing much talk of frequent flier programs, and seeing all fares changing together, is likely to feel that airline competition, like almost everything else, is not what it used to be. Although these and other aspects of airline travel undoubtedly affect consumer welfare, the effects are frequently small and are in no sense as large as the annual net benefits to travelers from deregulation. Based on the estimates in chapter 2 and this chapter, those annual benefits amount to $18.4 billion in 1993 dollars (table 4-13).

No doubt airlines are availing themselves of various strategies to limit competition. But at least so far the pressures of competition, and possibly the occasional regulatory intervention such as prohibiting display screen bias in reservation systems, are strictly limiting their success. The gains travelers have reaped from deregulation remain considerable.

Appendix

This appendix presents the technical analysis that underlies the causality tests and the estimation of the price-cost margins used to calculate the cost of price leadership to travelers. It also explains sensitivity tests of the conclusions obtained from the causality tests. Finally, it presents the calculation that underlies the estimate of the inconvenience costs to business travelers from travel restrictions under regulation.

Causality Tests

To test causality between two fare series, both must be stationary. Formally, $E(Y_t) = \mu$, $Var(Y_t) = \sigma^2$, and $Cov(Y_t, Y_{t-k}) = \gamma(k)$. Intuitively, these conditions mean that the series does not depend on time. The order of integration of a time series variable is the number of times the variable must be differenced before it becomes stationary. Thus if the series itself is stationary, it is said to be integrated of order zero, abbreviated I(0). If variable Y is not stationary, but the first-difference variable, $\Delta Y = Y_t - Y_{t-1}$, is stationary, the original series is integrated of order one, I(1). If the first-difference variable must be differenced before it is stationary, the original series is integrated of order two, I(2), and so on.

If a time series is not stationary it has one or more unit roots. An augmented Dickey-Fuller test is used to test for nonstationarity by testing for the presence of a unit root. To perform an augmented Dickey-Fuller test, the regression $\Delta Y_t = \alpha + \beta \; Trend + \gamma Y_{t-1} + \sum_{i=1}^{k} \delta_i \Delta Y_{t-i}$ is run, where *Trend* is a time trend term and k is the number of lagged first differences included in the equation. If the estimate of γ is negative and significantly different from zero, we reject the null hypothesis of a unit root in favor of the hypothesis that Y is stationary, I(0).[86] Intuitively, we are testing whether the change in Y is influenced by the level of Y. If it is not ($\gamma = 0$), a "jump" in Y will not be "corrected," and the mean of Y will be a function of time, violating a condition for stationarity. If, however, a large value of Y_{t-1} results in a relatively large negative ΔY, this implies $\gamma < 0$, that is, the series is reverting toward its original time-insensitive mean. If Y is not stationary, perhaps ΔY is. An analogous test

---

86. The estimate of γ does not have a t-distribution. Thus the test is not a t-test, but an augmented Dickey-Fuller test.

is the one in which Y is replaced by ΔY (that is, does the change in Y influence the change in the change of Y?).

In testing for causality between two series, the case in which both are integrated of the same order requires special treatment because it is possible that the series are cointegrated. Two series are cointegrated if some linear combination of them is stationary. This implies that the two original series have the same stochastic trend. To test for cointegration, one series is regressed on the other, a time trend, and a constant term. The residuals from this cointegrating regression are then tested for stationarity using the augmented Dickey-Fuller test (without the constant term and the time trend). If the null hypothesis that the residuals from the cointegrating regression are nonstationary can be rejected, the original series are cointegrated.[87]

Summary results (using average fares) for the augmented Dickey-Fuller tests are presented in table 4A-1 for three significance levels (the levels at which the null hypothesis of nonstationarity could be rejected).[88] The most common outcome is that the fare levels for each carrier in a competitive pair are integrated of order one (fare levels are not stationary, but fare changes are).[89] This is typical for many economic time series.

Of the 351 competitive pairs that were both integrated of order one at the 10 percent significance level, 69 (20 percent) were cointegrated (also using the 10 percent significance level). The results for the 5 percent and 1 percent significance levels were 13 percent (53 out of 400) and 4 percent (15 out of 344). These figures seem smaller than intuition would have predicted. The nature of air transportation, especially under deregulation, is that fare differences over time between carriers are likely to be stable, or simply zero. Our results may be due to two factors. First, the null hypothesis of the test for cointegration is that the series are not cointegrated. This means that evidence in support of cointegration must be very strong for a finding of cointegration to result. Second, even if all carriers charged the same fares, if the mix of travelers paying each fare varied across carriers over time, average fare differences between carriers need not be stationary.

87. If fares of the two carriers in the causation regression are cointegrated, the Granger causality test is changed somewhat. In addition to the fare variables, the lagged residual from the cointegrating regression is also included as a right-hand-side variable. Causality exists if the γ's are different from zero or if the coefficient of the lagged residuals is different from zero.

88. For this test we included one lagged first-difference term in the equation.

89. The results for twentieth, fiftieth, and eightieth percentile and for logs were similar.

Table 4A-1. *Results of Tests for Unit Roots for Average Fare*[a]

	Second competitor			
First competitor	I(0)	I(1)	I(2)	≥ I(3)
	1 percent significance level[b]			
I(0)	1.1	2.1	0.9	0.5
I(1)	2.7	42.1	11.3	3.1
I(2)	0.5	8.8	12.1	5.4
≥ I(3)	0.0	2.8	4.4	2.3
	5 percent significance level[b]			
I(0)	4.9	9.2	1.3	0.1
I(1)	6.2	49.0	7.6	2.1
I(2)	0.9	7.7	6.2	1.3
≥ I(3)	0.4	1.1	1.3	0.6
	10 percent significance level[b]			
I(0)	11.0	13.7	0.9	0.2
I(1)	10.3	43.0	5.8	1.5
I(2)	1.3	5.3	3.8	0.5
≥ I(3)	0.4	1.3	0.9	0.2

Source: Authors' calculations.
a. Percentage of 817 competitive pairs by order of integration of first competitor (row) and second competitor (column).
b. Significance level is the level at which the null hypothesis of the presence of unit roots can be rejected.

Having determined the order of integration and tested for cointegration, we tested for causality, limiting the test to those situations in which the fares of the two carriers in a competitive pair were both integrated of order zero or both of order one. Thus in the first case we asked whether knowledge of carrier A's past fare levels helped predict carrier B's current fare level, and vice versa. In the second case we asked whether knowledge of carrier A's past fare changes helped predict carrier B's current fare changes. Although it would have been statistically justified to test for causality for any order of integration of the underlying fares (as long as both variables used in the causal regressions were stationary), we believe that it did not make economic sense to do so.[90]

Of the 817 competitive pairs, both carriers' fares were I(1) for 351 pairs and I(0) for 90 pairs, resulting in causality tests run for 441 competitive pairs, which means 882 causality tests were run because causality

90. For example, table 4A-1 shows that for the 10 percent significance level in 24 percent (10.3 + 13.7) of competitive pairs, one carrier's fares are integrated of order one while the other's are integrated of order zero. To apply the causality test we would be asking whether one carrier's past fare changes affect another carrier's current fare levels (and whether one carrier's past fare levels affect the other carrier's current fare changes).

Table 4A-2. *Share of Causality Tests Exhibiting Granger Causality, Sensitivity of Findings*

Item	Average fare significance level			20th percentile fare significance level			50th percentile fare significance level			80th percentile fare significance level		
	10	*5*	*1*	*10*	*5*	*1*	*10*	*5*	*1*	*10*	*5*	*1*
Levels: 1 lag	24	17	6	26	19	8	22	15	6	29	20	9
Levels: 4 lags	8	5	1	10	5	2	8	5	1	11	7	4
Logs: 1 lag	24	16	6	27	18	8	21	15	5	27	19	8
Logs: 4 lags	7	3	1	10	6	2	6	5	1	9	5	3

Source: Authors' calculations.

must be tested in both directions (do A's fares cause B's fares and do B's fares cause A's fares). Results are not reported for any test that had fewer than twenty observations in the causal regression (with one lag). What remains is 806 causality tests covering 245 routes.

Sensitivity Tests

Table 4-8 presented the results of the causality tests for the base case using the average fare, a 10 percent significance level, and one lag. The findings on fare causality turned out to be robust for alternative specifications of the causality tests. The percentage of causality tests with a positive finding was not affected very much by the use of levels instead of logs or the choice of which part of the fare distribution to test (table 4A-2). As expected, a lower significance level and incorporating additional lags in the test made it easier to statistically reject causality.[91]

Price-Cost Margins

Our interest was in the difference between price-cost margins on routes where causation was found and those where it was not found; our interest was not in the level of price-cost margins on any route. Thus the following simple approach should have been adequate. We first simplified the analysis by choosing to calculate $(P - AC)/P$ (price-cost margin is usually defined as $(P - MC)/P$). To use even this simpler approach, one

---

91. When we report causality with four lags, we mean that causality was found with one, two, three, and four lags.

needs carrier- and route-specific costs, but estimating these costs from available data is difficult. We thus used an approach (paralleling that of James Brander and Anming Zhang) in which a carrier's route-specific costs are a function of the route's distance.[92]

We assumed that for each carrier the observed cost per passenger of serving a route was generated by the following equation: $C = A \cdot D^\theta$, where C is the cost per passenger, A is a constant, D is the route distance, and θ is the elasticity of cost with respect to distance. This implies that cost per passenger mile is $CPM = A \cdot D^{\theta-1}$, which implies $A = CPM \cdot D^{1-\theta}$. At the mean, $A = \overline{CPM} \cdot \overline{ASL}^{1-\theta}$, where $\overline{CPM}$ is a carrier's reported cost per passenger mile, and $\overline{ASL}$ is the carrier's average stage length (average flight distance).

We estimated θ by regressing the log of average real fare (for each carrier on each route on the most heavily traveled 1,000 routes for each quarter from the fourth quarter of 1978 to the fourth quarter of 1991 for which data were available) on the log of distance. The result was a value of θ equal to 0.539, which is reasonable in that fares increase with distance, although less than proportionally because of the fixed costs of takeoff and landing.

Given the expression for A and the value of θ and substituting, costs per passenger for carrier i on route j during time period t are

$$C_{i,j,t} = \overline{CPM}_{i,t} \cdot \overline{ASL}_{i,t}^{.461} \cdot D_j^{.539}.$$

$\overline{CPM}$ was calculated from airline cost data submitted by carriers to the Department of Transportation on form 41 using the costing methodology the department uses in calculating the standard industry fare level (SIFL).[93] The variable $\overline{ASL}_{i,t}$ was calculated from data on form 41 for domestic scheduled passenger service.

We compared average cost per passenger mile for our 1,000-route sample with carriers' overall cost per passenger mile (from form 41) and

92. James A. Brander and Anming Zhang, "Market Conduct in the Airline Industry: An Empirical Investigation," *Rand Journal of Economics*, vol. 21 (Winter 1990), pp. 567–83.

93. This involves estimating those expenses that can be attributed to scheduled passenger operations, given that carriers engage in scheduled and charter passenger operations as well as freight (property and mail) operations. We subtracted property and mail revenue, charter revenue (times 0.95, which assumes that charter operations would not take place unless they earned a profit), and transport-related expense (actually the lesser of transport-related revenues and transport-related expense) from operating expense to yield passenger operating expense, where all cost categories refer to domestic service.

found that overall costs were 16.7 percent higher than our estimated costs. This result may be due to several factors, perhaps the most important of which is our assuming, by necessity, that each route in our sample was operated nonstop when in some cases intermediate stops would have been made. Because costs rise less than proportionately with distance, the cost of, for example, two flights of length $D/2$ would be more than the cost of one flight of length D. Accordingly, we inflated all of our estimated costs by 16.7 percent. Once again, because we made no use of the absolute level of price-cost margins, but only their difference, this did not affect our results.

The Cost of Travel Restrictions during Regulation

Our estimate of the proportion of business travelers who suffered inconvenience costs from travel restrictions during regulation was obtained as follows. During regulation, 37 percent of all travelers flew under restrictions.[94] Unfortunately, this figure is not broken down by business and pleasure travel. But it has been estimated that during deregulation roughly 50 percent of business travelers fly under restrictions and nearly 100 percent of pleasure travelers do so. Thus we assumed the proportion of pleasure-restricted to business-restricted travel, 2:1, was the same under regulation as it is under deregulation and also that 50 percent of travel is for business and 50 percent of travel is for pleasure. Thus 48 percent of the pleasure travelers flew under restrictions during regulation, and 24 percent of the business travelers flew under restrictions.

There was then the question of what type of restrictions business travelers incur. According to our sample, 50 percent of the restricted business travelers during deregulation had a Saturday night stay restriction and advance reservation requirements. According to airline marketing executives, 80 to 90 percent of business travelers using discount fares traveled under Saturday night stay and advance reservation requirements during regulation because only a few types of restricted fares were offered. (We used the midpoint figure of 85 percent.) Thus the proportion of business travelers incurring costly restrictions under deregulation is 25 percent (50 percent incurring restrictions multiplied by 50 percent incurring the onerous restrictions estimated here), while the proportion of business travelers incurring costly restrictions under regulation is 20 per-

94. Air Transport Association, *Monthly Discount Reports* (various issues).

cent (24 percent multiplied by 85 percent). Thus the proportion of de-regulated to regulated business travelers incurring costly restrictions is 25 percent to 20 percent, or 1.25:1. Given the absence of corroborating or contradictory evidence, we assumed that the cost of a given restriction under regulation was the same as its cost under deregulation. Thus, ignoring trip generation effects, if deregulated business travelers suffered a $5 billion annual cost from the restrictions, regulated business travelers suffered a $4 billion annual cost ($5 billion divided by 1.25), for a net cost from deregulation of $1 billion (in 1990 dollars). Expressing this in 1993 dollars for comparability with our other estimates yields $1.1 billion.

To be sure, this estimate is sensitive to our assumptions. If, for example, the share of business travelers who suffered inconvenience costs during regulation was less than we estimated (perhaps 15 percent instead of 20 percent), then the costs of restrictions rise by another $1 billion, but this cost still represents a small percentage of the benefits from deregulation.

CHAPTER FIVE

Airline Profitability

FROM 1990 TO 1993 the U.S. airline industry lost billions of dollars, wiping out much of its net worth. Losses were not confined to a few poorly run carriers: nine of the ten largest lost money during some of those years. A number of carriers have gone into bankruptcy, and Pan American, Eastern, and Midway have been liquidated. The heavy losses have created widespread apprehension and led during the summer of 1993 to the creation of the National Commission to Ensure a Strong Competitive Airline Industry to study the situation.

To some extent policymakers face a dilemma. They agree that the industry must become more profitable if it is to continue to attract capital. But as chapter 4 noted, they continue to guard against airline practices that might increase fares. Thus before any policy to address the industry's financial problems can be considered, it is essential to understand the source of these problems. That is the focus of this chapter.

As the news media explain the airlines' financial problems, the industry is doomed to cutthroat competition and will never become profitable. Their argument is essentially that because the short-run marginal cost of air transportation is low and is lower than short-run average cost, competition will drive fares (equal to short-run marginal cost) down to unprofitable levels in the near term. However, as chapter 2 showed, the industry was profitable during the mid-1980s. Its recent losses began during the macroeconomic slowdown in the late 1980s and grew during the recession in the early 1990s, which has led some researchers to argue that industry profits track the business cycle. In particular, they contend that the industry loses money during periods of slow economic growth because it suffers from overcapacity as a result of poor economic forecasts.[1] Other explanations of the losses focus on the lower fares that

---

1. See, for example, John R. Meyer and Clinton V. Oster, Jr., with John S. Strong, "Airline Financial Performance since Deregulation," in John R. Meyer and Clinton V. Oster, Jr., eds., *Deregulation and the Future of Intercity Passenger Travel* (MIT Press, 1987), pp. 17–38, for a discussion of this problem in the context of the airline industry's financial problems during the early 1980s.

carriers allegedly have to charge when they compete against carriers in bankruptcy and when two carriers have repeated competitive contacts with one another on various routes during difficult economic times. The subject that is raised and investigated here is how carriers' fares, and ultimately their profits, are affected by the particular carriers they compete with in their markets.

The Cost of Forecast Errors

A common explanation of the industry's recent financial problems is overcapacity—too many seats chasing too few passengers. Between 1970 and 1985 the major airlines operated roughly 1,700 aircraft. From 1985 to 1990, in response to the 1980s expansion and their freedom to enter new markets, they expanded their fleets more than 76 percent to 3,000 aircraft, while passenger demand rose only 36 percent.[2]

An industry is likely to experience overcapacity if it makes excessively optimistic forecasts of economic growth. For example, Donald F. Barnett and Robert W. Crandall have pointed out that the steel industry has suffered from periodic episodes of overcapacity because of forecast errors.[3] Did that happen to the airline industry as well? Airlines must make their capacity decisions years in advance because of the time it takes to acquire new aircraft. Accordingly, they must make periodic forecasts of the economy to reduce the possibility that their decisions will result in excess or insufficient capacity. Economic forecasts are all the more essential because air travel is highly sensitive to changes in consumer income.[4] The potential for forecast errors is illustrated by American Airlines' 1989 growth plan, as stated by its chairman, Robert L. Crandall: "We see no reason, and very little likelihood, for there being a recession in the next five years, except bad governmental policy. And we're hoping we don't have bad governmental policy."[5]

---

2. The unpublished figures on total unstandardized industry fleet size are from Avmark, Inc., Rosslyn, Virginia. The figure for the change in passenger demand is based on an increase in revenue passenger miles from 336 billion in 1985 to 458 billion in 1990. These figures are from Air Transport Association, *Air Transport 1994: The Annual Report of the U.S. Scheduled Airline Industry* (Washington), p. 3.

3. Donald F. Barnett and Robert W. Crandall, *Up from the Ashes: The Rise of the Steel Minimill in the United States* (Brookings, 1986).

4. An income elasticity of around 1.5 is typically obtained from time-series analyses of aggregate air travel demand.

5. See Dan Reed, *The American Eagle: The Ascent of Bob Crandall and American Airlines* (St. Martin's Press, 1993), p. 238.

A simple calculation illustrates the potential consequences of forecast errors. Assuming an income elasticity of demand of 1.5, a real GDP forecast error that is overly optimistic by 5 percent would cause airlines to add 7.5 percent too much to capacity. Burdened with excess capacity, they would be forced by competition to lower their fares. Assuming a systemwide price elasticity of demand of -0.7, fares would fall by 10.7 percent (7.5 divided by 0.7) as carriers tried to fill the empty seats. After accounting for the 7.5 percent greater ridership that the lower fares would by design induce, revenue would decrease by 4.0 percent.[6] With annual passenger revenue approximately $60 billion, the forecast error would shrink industry profits by $2.4 billion.[7]

Although this calculation is plausible, corroborating empirical evidence of a link between forecast errors and industry profits is desirable. To measure this link, we needed some forecast from which to calculate the errors. We did not know what forecasting procedure the industry uses. Indeed, the industry does not forecast; each airline does its own forecast. Nonetheless, a simple procedure can be hypothesized to approximate aggregate industry forecasts and see whether the resulting errors can explain the profits actually observed. Of course, it would be desirable to develop and estimate a model of optimal airline investment in seating capacity, but the specification and data requirements are exceedingly difficult to achieve. A standard neoclassical investment model, however, shows that expected growth in output has a critical influence on investment. Our approach to analyzing investment focuses on the link between predictions of national output (GDP) and industry profitability, but we also show how the accuracy of these predictions affects investments in seating capacity.

We forecast GDP m years in the future using actual GDP growth during the previous n years. Because we did not know the appropriate values of m (the lead) or n (the lag), we generated forecasts using all thirty combinations of three leads (from one to three years) and ten lags (from one to ten years). We then calculated thirty forecast error series in percentages, one for each lag-lead combination, and used each of these

6. Because fares are 10.7 percent lower and quantity is 7.5 percent higher, revenue is $(1 - 0.107) \times (1 + 0.075) = 0.96$ times what it would be without forecast errors (a 4 percent decline).

7. Because carriers have as much capacity and carry as many passengers as they would have had their forecasts been correct, costs are the same regardless of the actual performance of the economy. Thus the fare cuts to fill capacity that reduce revenue by $2.4 billion also reduce profits by the same amount.

Figure 5-1. *Predicted GDP Minus Actual GDP, Eight-Year Lag, Two-Year Lead, 1950–93*

Percent of actual GDP

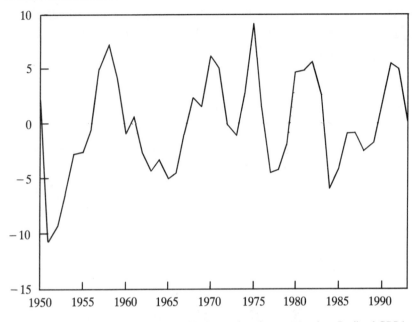

Source: Authors' calculations using national income and product accounts data. Predicted GDP is based on an extrapolation two years into the future using the average growth rate in GDP during the previous eight years.

series in separate regressions to see which best explained industry gross profit margins.[8] We found that an eight-year lag and a two-year lead were best (based on corrected R^2). This seemed a plausible basis for forecasts because eight years is roughly the duration of a business cycle and two years is a reasonable time for ordering and receiving new aircraft. Figure 5-1 shows the forecast errors of GDP corresponding to this lag-lead structure. A positive forecast error means that actual GDP was lower than predicted. To the extent that our forecasting procedure matched the results of aggregate industry forecasts, it is clear that the industry has periodically made forecast errors and most recently overestimated economic growth.[9]

8. Gross profit margin is profit before taxes and interest on long-term debt expressed as a percentage of revenue.

9. As an alternative to our forecasting procedure, we tried to use nonpolitical consensus

Using our best estimate of the forecast errors, we then estimated the effect the errors had on industry profits by regressing industry gross profit margins on them, allowing for the effects to vary according to whether the industry was regulated or deregulated and allowing for profits to depend also on GDP growth directly.[10] The results from a regression using data from 1951 to 1993 are (standard errors in parentheses):

$$gross\ profit\ margin\ =\ 3.452$$
$$(1.609)$$

$$-\ 0.369\ (forecast\ error\ during\ regulation)$$
$$(0.130)$$

$$-\ 0.560\ (forecast\ error\ during\ deregulation)$$
$$(0.162)$$

$$+\ 0.120\ (GDP\ growth)$$
$$(0.131)$$

$$\rho\ =\ 0.797;\ DW\ statistic\ =\ 1.80$$
$$(0.099)$$

$$\bar{R}^2\ =\ .77;\ N\ =\ 42.$$

The forecast errors have a statistically significant effect on the gross profit margins.[11] Overpredictions of GDP reduce profits; underpredictions increase them.[12] The effect is greater under deregulation, although

---

forecasts. Unfortunately, we were not able to find one that extended far enough back in time and that forecasted far enough into the future to be useful.

10. We also used net profit margin with little effect on the results. Nor were the results affected by alternative specifications that included fuel price, which was insignificant, and various time trends.

11. One must be careful in stating that the forecast errors have a statistically significant effect on profits, because the forecast error equation was chosen from a number of competing lag and lead structures on the basis of how well it predicted profits. We also found, however, that the forecast errors generated by competing structures had a statistically significant effect on profits.

12. We also tried a specification where the effect of forecast errors was allowed to vary according to whether the forecast error was positive or negative and according to regulatory regime. The difference between the resulting coefficients for positive and negative errors was very small (0.05 during regulation and −0.07 during deregulation) and not statistically significant.

the difference is not statistically significant.[13] GDP growth has a positive but statistically imprecise effect on profits.[14] During deregulation a 1 percent overestimate of GDP reduces the gross profit margin by 0.56 percentage points. Multiplying this coefficient by the forecast error in 1992 (4.94 percent) times 1992 industry revenues yields a loss to the industry of $2.2 billion. Performing this calculation for 1990, 1991, and 1993 yields losses of $0.8 billion, $2.3 billion, and zero. Thus the cost to the industry caused by poor forecasts of the economy from 1990 to 1993 could be $5.3 billion.[15]

What share of the industry's total losses during this period might be accounted for by forecast errors? If carriers had earned a 12 percent rate of return based on the amount of long-term debt and stockholders' equity, aggregate gross profit from 1990 to 1993 would have been $12.1 billion, leaving a $16.8 billion gap between the actual return (− $4.7 billion) and the 12 percent return. Forecast errors appear to account for about one-third of the profit gap.

But this simple calculation represents a substantial underestimate. First, the target 12 percent rate of return is too high. Although fares were set during regulation to achieve this rate, the best the industry has earned in any four-year period since 1968 is an average rate of 9.7 percent, and the average rate in the ten years before deregulation (1968 to 1977) was 5.1 percent. Using these two figures lowers annual target profits to $9.8 billion and $5.1 billion, respectively, instead of $12.1 billion, and shrinks the profit gap to $14.5 billion and $9.8 billion, respectively, instead of $16.8 billion. Second, as pointed out in chapter 2, note 24, four carriers that were in bankruptcy during this period accounted for substantial losses ($3.4 billion in operating profits). Subtracting these unusual losses closes the profit gap to $11.1 billion and $6.4 billion, depending on which target rate of return is used. Thus the $5.3 billion in

13. The effect could be greater under deregulation because the industry is free to raise fares when capacity is scarce, while competition prevents the industry from effectively engaging in cartel behavior when there is excess capacity. But under deregulation firms have more freedom to adjust routes, fares, and other aspects of operations to mitigate the effect of any unforeseen events.

14. The results did not change very much when we dropped GDP growth from the specification.

15. It is easy to show that the profit difference because of forecast error (equal to the revenue difference because of constant cost—see note 7) equals the predicted change in gross margin times actual revenue divided by one minus predicted margin. However, because margins are so small, this adjustment lowers the cost of forecast errors from 1990 to 1993 by only $3 million.

industry losses in 1990–93 that are due to forecast errors accounts for 48 percent of the profit gap when measured against the industry's best four-year performance since 1968 and 83 percent of the gap when measured against its average performance from 1968 to 1977. And a final adjustment to account for the effect of the fear of terrorism on the demand for air travel during the period of tensions in the Middle East and the Gulf War would close the profit gap still more and expand the forecast errors' responsibility for it even further.

This exercise alone cannot prove that industry executives made forecasting errors or that they invested in too much capacity. An airline investment model could potentially provide more persuasive evidence. But the justification for this conclusion can also be substantially strengthened by establishing an empirical link between forecast errors and industry excess capacity. We therefore regressed industry excess capacity for 1951 to 1993 as measured by the percentage of empty seats (one minus the industry load factor) on a constant and our measure of industry forecast error. We found that forecast errors had a statistically significant effect on excess capacity: a 5 percentage point error increased excess capacity by 1 percentage point.[16] Thus while the airlines' forecasting procedure may differ from ours, our methodology generated forecast errors that plausibly tracked the business cycle and predicted operating losses and excess capacity consistent with observed financial performance. Given that overcapacity is widely considered a problem in the airline industry, it is likely that forecast errors are a major source of the problem.[17]

The Determinants of Individual Airline Profitability

Despite the likelihood of industrywide forecast errors, some carriers have been able to weather financial crises better than others. We sought to understand why by examining the determinants of carriers' rates of return from 1970 to 1988.[18] We tried to extend the analysis into the early

16. The true effect of forecast errors on excess capacity is likely to be greater than we have estimated because airlines take actions to mask excess capacity, such as parking aircraft in the desert, canceling leases, reducing aircraft utilization, and lowering fares to fill planes.

17. It might be argued that the industry could have quickly unloaded excess capacity in the used aircraft market. However, the potential buyers of this aircraft, primarily foreign carriers, were also suffering from overcapacity during this period.

18. The rate of return for each major U.S. carrier was calculated by subtracting operating expenses, depreciation (the change in market value) of aircraft, and depreciation of

1990s, but we encountered parameter instability, probably because of changing plans of air travelers and carrier and route disruptions caused by Middle East tensions and subsequent conflict, slower growth of the economy, and the sharp increase in airline capacity.[19]

Our investigation applied the framework Ann F. Friedlaender, Ernst R. Berndt, and Gerard McCullough used to study companies' performance in the railroad industry.[20] The approach was to estimate a structural model of carriers' rates of return and then simulate the effect of various influences on profitability by estimating how the profits of the most profitable airlines would be affected if they had the characteristics of the least profitable airlines and vice versa. It was necessary to use a structural model because some of the endogenous variables in the model were characteristics used in the simulations, and we therefore needed to account for their effects directly.

The influences on carriers' rates of return included input costs, fares, network and operating characteristics, and managerial characteristics.[21] Input costs, which should decrease rates of return, included average employee compensation, fuel price, and maintenance expenses. The average fare, which should increase rates of return, was also included in the specification.[22] Network and operating characteristics were the share

---

nonflight equipment from airline revenue (less subsidy, which represents a tiny fraction of revenue). The resulting figure was divided by the market value of assets. Market value of aircraft and depreciation of aircraft were obtained from Avmark, Inc. All other data are from the Department of Transportation, form 41. We were not estimating a neoclassical profit function and thus did not include an opportunity cost of capital in total cost. In addition, the rate of return model was not bound by restrictions concerning returns to scale. There are no publicly available data on the market value of slots and gates, but the profits from selling these are generally small. In addition, booking fees from computer reservation systems were included in the revenue for those airlines that own a CRS. They were not included in revenues if the holding company, but not the airline, owned the CRS. Finally, changes in unclaimed frequent flier miles were accounted for.

19. There were other recessionary periods in our sample, but none of them were accompanied by declines in travel because of fears of terrorism.

20. Ann F. Friedlaender, Ernst R. Berndt, and Gerard McCullough, "Governance Structure, Managerial Characteristics, and Firm Performance in the Deregulated Rail Industry," *Brookings Papers on Economic Activity: Microeconomics* (1992), pp. 95–186.

21. Initial estimations also included fixed carrier effects, time effects, and macroeconomic variables, but these variables were insignificant and did not lead to any material changes in the results. The macroeconomic variables did not vary by carrier, which may explain their weak statistical effect. Finally, using a Chow test, we did not reject parameter stability during the change in regulatory policy.

22. We expected a positive effect because we were estimating the effect of average fare on rates of return, holding load factor constant.

of a carrier's enplanements at hub airports, average length of haul, average load factor, route density, and a dummy variable indicating whether a carrier developed and managed a computer reservation system.[23] As discussed in chapter 4, airlines can potentially use hubs and computer reservation systems to increase market share; higher load factors, greater route densities, and longer lengths of haul increase operating efficiency. Thus these variables should have increased a carrier's rate of return. Managerial characteristics, specified for the president and first vice president, included length of employment with the carrier, years of previous airline industry experience, and education.[24] These characteristics should in all likelihood have increased rates of return.

Because several of the variables could be endogenous, we conducted specification tests and rejected the exogeneity of fare, average load factor, and route density.[25] But we did not reject the exogeneity of the managerial characteristics. Although the finding that airline management (and thus their characteristics) is not systematically influenced by airline profitability may seem counterintuitive, it may simply be a manifestation of the separation of ownership and control common to large corporations. Given this separation, bad managers may persist—or be replaced by others with the same characteristics—in the airline industry as in any other.[26]

Estimation results are presented in table 5-1.[27] The coefficients have their expected sign, and most are estimated with reasonable statistical

23. It would be desirable to control for the size of a carrier's CRS measured by the number of tickets nationwide that are booked on it. Unfortunately, this information is not publicly available.

24. These characteristics were also used by Friedlaender, Berndt, and McCullough, "Governance Structure, Managerial Characteristics, and Firm Performance." We also included the managers' ages and a dummy variable signifying whether they had earned a college degree, but these variables were insignificant. *President* and *vice president* refer to the two highest corporate managers. In some cases, these were the CEO and the president. We also specified the characteristics of the third ranking manager (the *second vice president* in our terminology), but these characteristics were insignificant.

25. We used a Hausman specification test. The instruments included GNP, disposable income, interest rates, a deregulation dummy variable, carrier dummy variables, and other exogenous variables in the model. The basic conclusions from our analysis were not particularly sensitive to changes in which instruments to include.

26. See Severin Borenstein, "The Evolution of U.S. Airline Competition," *Journal of Economic Perspectives*, vol. 6 (Spring 1992), pp. 45–73.

27. Because the exogenous variables are used as instruments to estimate the included endogenous variables, one must exercise caution in interpreting and comparing the actual magnitudes of the coefficients because the true effect of a given exogenous variable also includes its effect on the included endogenous variables.

Table 5-1. *Estimated Effects of Airline Industry Factors and Other Factors on Airlines' Annual Rates of Return, 1970–88*[a]

Variable	Coefficient
Constant	−1.6789
	(0.5569)
Average fare (cents per mile)	0.0637
	(0.0182)
Average compensation (thousand dollars per employee)	−0.0070
	(0.0031)
Fuel price (dollars per gallon)	−0.2661
	(0.1047)
Maintenance expense (millions of dollars	−0.0550
per aircraft)	(0.0296)
Share of total enplanements at hub airports (percent)	0.0013
	(0.0030)
1978–83 CRS dummy (1 if carrier developed and managed a	0.0140
CRS 1978–83, 0 otherwise)	(0.0362)
1984–88 CRS dummy (1 if carrier developed and managed a	0.0700
CRS 1984–88, 0 otherwise)	(0.0349)
Average length of haul (thousands of miles)	0.3119
	(0.1502)
Average load factor (percent)	0.0147
	(0.0047)
Route density (passenger miles divided by route miles)	0.0037
	(0.0026)
President's total years with the airline	0.0043
	(0.0016)
President's total years of previous work experience in the	0.0063
airline industry	(0.0033)
President's education dummy (1 if president obtained a	0.0408
business degree, 0 otherwise)	(0.0236)
Vice president's total years with the airline	0.0017
	(0.0009)
Vice president's education dummy (1 if vice president obtained a	0.0372
business or law degree, 0 otherwise)	(0.0244)

Sources: All appropriate variables were put in real terms (1989 dollars) using a GDP inflator and a CPI fuel index for fuel price. Fuel price, average compensation, maintenance expense, and enplanement data were provided by the Air Transport Association. Information on computer reservation systems was supplied by individual carriers. Average fare, average length of haul, average load factor, and route density were computed from Department of Transportation, *Traffic Data of Certificated Route Air Carriers* (various issues). Because of the lack of published data, route miles was approximated. One estimate is given by $\frac{1}{2} n (n-1) \cdot$ *average length of haul*, where n is the number of cities served. This approximation is exact if all possible routes in the network are used with equal traffic flows. A lower-bound estimate is given by $(n \cdot$ *average length of haul*). A final estimate is the average of the two preceding estimates. The estimated results in the table are based on the final approximation. Use of the other approximations had little effect on the estimated coefficient of route density. All management variables are from Dun and Bradstreet, *Reference Book of Corporate Management* (New York, various years).

a. $\overline{R}^2 = .62$; number of observations = 159. Heteroskedastic-consistent standard errors are in parentheses. Estimation corrected for the unbalanced panel that was created because a few carriers were not included for the entire sample period, since they had incomplete rate-of-return information at the starting date of the sample.

precision. A primary finding is that the characteristics of a carrier's network appear to be more important to its financial success than either its size or the concentration of its traffic at hubs. The economies from higher load factors, longer lengths of haul, and greater route densities, which can be achieved by small and large airlines alike, have a significant effect on rates of return. Variables related only to size that were included in initial estimations—number of cities served, total departures, and so on—and the concentration of a carrier's enplanements at a hub, included for illustrative purposes, were statistically insignificant.

One competitive advantage that large carriers may have is their computer reservation systems, although it has taken time for this advantage to develop. The source of the high financial return implied by the 1984–88 CRS dummy, however, is controversial. The coefficient for this dummy implies that, all else constant, developing and managing a CRS adds 7 percentage points to a carrier's rate of return. This interpretation is misleading because, as indicated before, the CRS dummy is part of the set of instruments used to estimate the endogenous variables—average fare, average load factor, and route density—that were included. When its full effects are accounted for, the increase in the rate of return from a CRS is about 2.5 percentage points, much less than implied by its individual coefficient, but still important.[28]

This return may be considered an appropriate reward for a risky investment whose development costs are estimated to be more than $100 million. But the systems may also generate high returns for reasons unrelated to their owners' product development skills. First, as discussed in chapter 4, the systems have allegedly diverted many travelers to airlines that own a CRS. But our findings on the cost of the systems' bias suggest that with the exception of American Airlines the gains from traffic diversion are modest. Second, also as noted in chapter 4, note 49, CRS owners allegedly charge other airlines excessive booking fees to use their system. Our coefficient, however, could not capture this possibility completely because our rates of return included revenues from systems owned by airlines but not revenues from those owned by holding companies (for

28. CRSs do earn high rates of return. According to the Office of the Secretary of Transportation, *Study of Airline Computer Reservation Systems*, DOT-P-37-88-2 (Department of Transportation, May 1988), table 4.12, the rate of return (net income as a percent of investment) for the five CRSs in 1985 and 1986 ranged from −3.2 percent to 90.6 percent, with a collective rate of return (summed over all systems) of 50.4 percent in 1985 and 48.8 percent in 1986.

Table 5-2. *Average Annual Changes in Three Least Profitable Airlines'*
Profits If They Had Characteristics of Three Most Profitable Airlines,
1980–88
Millions of 1989 dollars

Characteristic	Least profitable airlines		
	Continental	Eastern	Pan American
Actual average annual profit, 1980–88	53.21	78.68	−90.95
Change in profit with			
USAir management[a]	28.49	107.34	75.02
Delta management[a]	56.52	163.03	113.13
American management[a]	24.97	89.40	62.35
USAir input costs[b]	−25.52	−64.38	−125.10
Delta input costs[b]	35.92	72.48	−30.07
American input costs[b]	30.81	57.75	−40.31
USAir operating characteristics[c]	70.09	152.57	244.31
Delta operating characteristics[c]	−50.21	−76.26	78.57
American operating characteristics[c]	74.27	186.99	263.78
USAir computer reservation system	0	−5.04	0
Delta computer reservation system	49.79	71.56	55.92
American computer reservation system	46.23	50.23	40.75

Source: Authors' calculations using data described in text.
a. Includes president's and vice president's experience and education as specified in table 5-1.
b. Includes fuel price, average compensation, and maintenance expenses as specified in table 5-1.
c. Includes average length of haul, average load factor, and route density as specified in table 5-1.

example, Sabre is actually owned by AMR, a holding company, not by
American Airlines). We speculated that the main benefit of a CRS is the
knowledge it gives a carrier about its potential customers' preferences
and the strength of demand in specific markets. As a result, a carrier's
yield management—its ability to determine the combination of seats to
be made available at a given fare class and the fare in that class that will
maximize revenue on a given flight—improves.

A final ingredient for success in the airline industry, according to our
findings, is an experienced management team with a business education.
For an airline president, experience with that airline and the industry are
important. Such experience is less important for the vice president, although experience with the airline has some statistical significance.

How much does management matter? Table 5-2 presents the results
of simulations that predicted how the three least profitable airlines from
1980 to 1988 (Continental, Eastern, and Pan American) would have fared
if they had had various characteristics of the three most profitable (USAir,

Delta, and American). This simulation captured the direct effect of a set of variables and their indirect effect as instruments for the endogenous variables. The average annual profits of Continental, Eastern, and Pan American would have grown substantially if they had had management like that of the top three, particularly Delta, which appears to have developed a management team with especially desirable characteristics.[29]

The results may raise the question of whether the best airline managers are underpaid. This is difficult to address because one must ask and analyze what would, for example, Delta's rate of return have been if its management had been replaced by the next best managerial team that could have been recruited? Using the managerial characteristics of the least profitable airlines to answer this question would be misleading. Undoubtedly, important personal considerations also enter into management compensation and retention. The chief executive at Continental Airlines, for example, was allegedly forced out by Continental's chairman despite bringing the carrier out of bankruptcy and seeing it report its first profit in a year. And the chairman of Alaska Airlines was forced to resign despite the company's reporting a profit for 1994. These considerations help explain why managerial characteristics are exogenous in a rate-of-return model.

As table 5-2 shows, superior management is the only consistent advantage that the most profitable carriers have over the least profitable ones.[30] USAir had higher input costs than the least profitable carriers, Pan American had lower input costs than the most profitable carriers, and Delta had less desirable operating characteristics than Continental and Eastern. The least profitable carriers would have benefited from American's and Delta's computer reservation systems. Interestingly, the gains, which would have reflected bias, better yield management, and to some extent booking fees, were more than double these carriers' losses from CRS bias (see chapter 4). Consequently, revenues generated from improved yield management appear to be the greatest benefit of owning a computer reservation system.

29. These findings did not derive from the influence of any one particular characteristic such as business education. All characteristics had an important influence.

30. Even with better managers Eastern would have probably had to grapple with labor problems and Pan American would have had to overcome a poor route structure. And it has turned out that even the airlines with the best managers lost a lot of money during the early 1990s. With better managers, however, the worst carriers would have performed better than they did, and without these managers the best carriers would have performed worse than they did.

A final matter is the effect of deregulation on industry profitability. Drawing on the experience from deregulation as of 1983, we found in earlier work that annual airline profits were $2.5 billion (in 1977 dollars) greater under deregulation than they would have been had the industry still been regulated.[31] We have updated this evaluation by comparing industry profits in 1988, the most recent year in our sample, with what they would have been if the industry had still been regulated. Because the U.S. economy was at comparable stages in the business cycle in 1978 and 1988, we used 1978, the last year airlines were regulated, as the year from which we predicted 1988 regulated profits.[32]

The approach we took was to make plausible adjustments to the variables in the rate-of-return model so their values reflected a 1988 regulated airline environment. We then used the model to predict 1988 regulated rates of return and converted these to 1988 regulated profits. We obtained an estimate of the 1988 regulated average fare by updating the standard industry fare level (SIFL) used in chapter 2 to predict regulated fares during the deregulated era. Turning to the factor prices, we assumed regulatory policy had no influence on fuel prices or maintenance expenses, so those variables kept their actual 1988 value. But 1988 average compensation was increased by 3 percent to reflect the effect of regulation on workers' earnings.[33]

The operating characteristics prevailing during regulation in 1978—average length of haul, average load factor, and route density—were used for the regulated 1988 values of these variables. This adjustment could be questioned on the grounds that these values could have increased during the decade despite the presence of regulation. But average length of haul and route density increased only a little in the period preceding deregulation, and although load factor did increase substantially, some

31. Steven Morrison and Clifford Winston, *The Economic Effects of Airline Deregulation* (Brookings, 1986), p. 40. This conclusion was also reached by Jose A. Gomez-Ibanez, Clinton V. Oster, Jr., and Don H. Pickrell, "Airline Deregulation: What's Behind the Recent Losses?" *Journal of Policy Analysis and Management*, vol. 3 (Winter 1983), pp. 74–89.

32. Both economies were in a period of mature expansion and experiencing stable growth. Capacity utilization, corporate profits as a share of GNP, and unemployment were slightly higher in 1978 than 1988.

33. This assumption is based on one set of findings in David Card, "Deregulation and Labor Earnings in the Airline Industry," Department of Economics, Princeton University, May 1989. Nancy Brown Johnson, "Airline Workers' Earnings and Union Expenditures under Deregulation," *Industrial Labor Relations Review*, vol. 45 (October 1991), pp. 154–65, also finds deregulation led to a small loss in airline workers' earnings.

of the increase was undoubtedly due to the effect of administrative fare deregulation. As such, the actual 1978 regulated load factor was only a few percentage points less than the actual 1988 deregulated load factor, which if anything suggests that our adjustment had led to an inflated 1988 regulated load factor. Although it was likely that the change in the regulatory environment did affect the share of hub enplanements, it was not clear how this variable should be adjusted. Thus we used its actual 1988 value for the 1988 regulated environment. But this procedure is likely to be innocuous because the share of hub enplanements had a weak effect on rates of return.

As pointed out in chapter 4, the advance of computer power rather than the change in regulatory policy spurred the development of computer reservation systems. Thus it was reasonable to use the actual 1988 value of the CRS dummy for the 1988 regulated environment. Finally, we were not aware of any evidence that the change in regulatory policy had affected managerial characteristics. As implied previously, the separation of ownership and management could have been a dominant factor in the lack of turnover in response to the change in the regulatory environment. Thus the actual 1988 values of the managerial characteristics were also used for the 1988 regulatory environment.

Making these adjustments to the variables in the rate-of-return model, we found that if the industry had still been regulated in 1988, fares would have been higher, but higher wages and less efficient operations would have more than offset those gains.[34] The carriers in our sample would have lost $1.47 billion as against actual 1988 profits of $0.56 billion. Thus they gained $2.03 billion from deregulation, and the annual gain from deregulation for the entire industry amounted to $2.6 billion in 1988 dollars.[35] That gain is understated because some administrative deregulation occurred before 1978 and because the initial phases of deregulation began in the final quarter of 1978.

Thus the evidence, based on two points in the business cycle, the early and later 1980s, is that deregulation led to higher profits.[36] This conclu-

34. Using data up through 1986, Badi H. Baltagi, James M. Griffin, and Daniel P. Rich, "Airline Deregulation: The Cost Pieces of the Puzzle," *International Economic Review*, vol. 36 (February 1995), pp. 245–58, found that deregulation lowered airlines' costs.

35. The carriers in the sample account for 78 percent of total industry profits. Thus we divided our sample estimate by 0.78 to obtain the industry estimate reported in the text.

36. The large losses during the early 1990s do not alter this conclusion because they appear to have been largely caused by poor forecasts during a recessionary period—factors

sion may seem surprising: shouldn't greater competition hold down profits? What happened? The most likely explanation is that with less incentive because of fare regulation and less opportunity to minimize costs, carriers' load factors and route densities were lower under regulation, their lengths of haul shorter, and their labor expenses higher than in an unregulated environment. Deregulation gave them more opportunities to profit, even in the face of increased competition, by giving them more freedom to differentiate fares by cost of service, more freedom to abandon unprofitable routes, more freedom to enter profitable routes, and more incentive to make more efficient use of labor and capital.

Bankruptcy, Multimarket Contact, and Industry Profitability

Industry profitability could be compromised when some carriers compete under adverse circumstances. For example, American and United Airlines, among others, have claimed that they are put at a severe disadvantage when they compete in markets with a carrier that is in bankruptcy. They have argued that bankrupt carriers slash their fares to fill their planes and keep cash flowing in to stave off their creditors. This action forces other carriers to lower their fares too. As a result of this pricing-for-cash strategy, the cash flow of the entire industry suffers. Industry profitability may also drop when two airlines compete vigorously against each other on many routes. In bad economic times this multimarket contact could expand the scope and cost of fare wars for the entire industry.

We calculated the effect on carrier revenue assuming, for simplicity, that there was no increased demand (and thus no increased cost) from the reductions in fares that resulted from competing against a bankrupt carrier or from multimarket contact. In the appendix to this chapter we derive a formula we used to adjust the figures in our tables for possible increased demand and cost to obtain an estimate of the effect that bankruptcy and multimarket contact have on profits. As explained in the appendix, the adjustment factor is 0.44 for the analysis on bankruptcy and 1.00 for the multimarket contact analysis. Thus the unadjusted change in revenues that we present can be viewed as upper bounds for

that are not inherently related to deregulation. Indeed, at the Airline Commission hearings held during the summer of 1993, airline industry executives strongly opposed a return to regulation.

the likely effect on profits. With the formula in the appendix, our figures can be adjusted using any demand and cost elasticity desired.

Bankrupt Carriers

Going into bankruptcy could easily encourage an airline to reduce its fares. First, with little left to lose and living day to day, management might take more risks, one of which could be trying to raise cash by slashing fares even without knowing how competitors will respond. Second, bankruptcy could also increase an airline's willingness to sacrifice future profits for current profits. With the future profits less important, the carrier could make decisions for today, putting off maintenance, ignoring depreciation, and postponing pension fund contributions and other labor expenses and interest and capital expenses. These moves effectively decrease the airline's marginal costs of production, also enabling it to lower fares. Finally, a bankrupt carrier is likely to suffer decreased demand as it reduces service and its reputation falters. Reducing fares helps offset this effect.

The justification for allowing a company to reorganize under Chapter 11 is to give it additional time to pay off its creditors, but to do so as a viable company. The airline industry has become concerned, however, that carriers have been allowed to spend too much time in bankruptcy and that the low fares they charged have drained the industry's revenues.

We used a fare equation to quantify the effect on industry revenues of competing against bankrupt carriers.[37] Because this is the policy-related matter of interest, we did not concern ourselves with the period before a carrier filed for bankruptcy, when their pricing strategy could have been attributed to a range of factors independent of their impending Chapter 11 status. For the same reason, we did not examine the effect of bankruptcy on carriers that remained in a market after a bankrupt carrier left. If bankruptcy caused a carrier to leave several of its markets, the carriers that remained—although presumably better off from the exit of a competitor—were not included in our analysis.

---

37. Bankruptcy can, of course, affect advertising expenditures, service, and other things as well as industry revenues. However, the effect of bankruptcy on other airline activities is difficult to quantify and less important to the public debate over whether bankrupt carriers have been a significant drain on industry revenues. It has also been argued that carriers have gone into bankruptcy to break up unions. See James Ott, "Unions Attack Continental, Eastern Moves," *Aviation Week and Space Technology*, October 10, 1983, pp. 32–33.

The distinctive feature of this application is that we estimated an equation for each airline that identified the effect on its fares of market contact with a carrier in bankruptcy, with all other influences being held constant. As in the baseline fare specification, these influences included route distance, route concentration, airport concentration, and route traffic density. We also included carrier-specific dummies. It is important to control for both contact regardless of bankruptcy status and contact with a carrier in bankruptcy status. It could be, for example, that American Airlines had lower fares in markets in which it competed with America West even when America West was not operating under Chapter 11. Failure to control for this effect through contact dummies would have led to biased estimates of the effect of bankrupt carriers on the fares of healthy carriers. Market presence and market contact were defined in an identical manner. We defined a carrier as serving a market if it carried more than one hundred sampled passengers during a particular quarter.[38] Thus both the carrier of interest and the bankrupt carrier had to have more than one hundred sampled passengers during a quarter on a particular route for route contact to have occurred. Our sample included quarterly data for the most heavily traveled 1,000 domestic routes as measured in 1990, some with and some without bankrupt carriers, from the fourth quarter of 1978 to the third quarter of 1992.

Estimation proceeded with bankruptcy dummies defined for eight major occurrences beginning with the first Continental Airlines bankruptcy in 1983. (Estimation results for key parameters are given in table 5A-1 in the appendix to this chapter.)[39] The effect of each bankruptcy on industry and carrier revenue is summarized in tables 5-3 and 5-4.[40]

38. Because the ticket sample is a 10 percent quarterly sample, 100 sampled passengers a quarter translates into about 75 passengers a week—about one flight a week.

39. We ran fourteen regressions, one for each carrier (the ten largest carriers in 1993, plus four others that had operated in bankruptcy and later exited the industry). For each regression the dependent variable was the log of that carrier's average fare for each of the 1,000 most heavily traveled routes it served. The independent variables were fifty-six quarterly time period dummy variables for each of the periods from the fourth quarter of 1978 to the third quarter of 1992, as many as thirteen carrier contact dummies (depending on the number of carriers that the carrier had some contact with), as many as eight bankruptcy contact dummies, and four variables in logs measuring distance, number of route passengers, number of effective competitors on the route, and the minimum number of effective competitors at the two airports that define the route.

40. Because our dependent variable was the log of average fare, the percentage by which contact with a given bankrupt carrier B changes carrier A's fares (relative to contact with that same carrier when it is not in bankruptcy and relative to current fares) is given

Table 5-3. *Estimated Effect of Airline Bankruptcies on Industry Revenue, by Bankrupt Airline, 1983–93*
Billions of dollars

Bankruptcy	Revenue change	Bankruptcy	Revenue change
Continental(1), September 1983–September 1986	−2.151	Midway, March 1991– November 1991[a]	−0.068
Eastern, March 1989– January 1991[a]	0.536	America West, June 1991– August 1994[b]	0.659
Braniff(2), September 1989– November 1989[a]	−0.018	TWA, February 1992– November 1993[b]	−0.963
Continental(2), December 1990–April 1993[b]	1.942	Total	−0.508
Pan American, January 1991– December 1991[a]	−0.444	Total since 1989	1.643

Source: Authors' calculations. Base case: greater than one-hundred sampled passengers; all point estimates used regardless of statistical significance. Bankruptcy dates provided by newspaper accounts compiled by authors.
a. Bankruptcy ended with liquidation.
b. Bankruptcy ended after the last period included in this analysis (third quarter 1992).

The tables present our base case, which uses all the estimated bankruptcy coefficients (regardless of statistical significance) and includes markets with at least one hundred sampled passengers a quarter. The effect of bankrupt carriers on revenues of other carriers has been small. The industry lost only $0.5 billion in revenue as a result of all the major bankruptcies since 1983 (table 5-3). However, bankruptcy can also weaken a carrier by tarnishing its image and allow the healthy competitors to raise fares. It turns out that this effect has been larger since 1989; the industry actually gained a net $1.6 billion from bankruptcies. The occurrence most costly to the industry was the first Continental bankruptcy, in which the relatively healthy carrier allegedly entered Chapter 11 to void labor contracts. Continental's second bankruptcy was different and apparently left the airline so weak that its major competitors were able to raise fares and increase revenues. As the appendix to this chapter

by $1 - \exp(-COEF)$, where $COEF$ is the regression coefficient of the bankruptcy dummy for carrier B in carrier A's fare regression. For each year carrier B was in bankruptcy, this expression was multiplied by the percentage of revenue earned by carrier A on routes on which it competes with carrier B (on the top 1,000 routes averaged over the period that carrier B was in bankruptcy) and by carrier A's domestic passenger revenue for each year (or fraction thereof, when a bankruptcy extended over less than a full year). As noted in the text, this calculation assumes no demand response. Adjustment factors for alternative demand and cost elasticities are given in the appendix to this chapter.

Table 5-4.   *Estimated Effect of Airline Bankruptcies on Revenues, by Airline Affected*
Billions of dollars

Affected carrier	Revenue change	Revenue change since 1989	Affected carrier	Revenue change	Revenue change since 1989
American	−0.220	−0.043	Midway	−0.009	−0.009
Alaska	0.009	0.030	Northwest	−0.102	−0.014
Braniff	0.000	0.000	Pan American	−0.051	−0.019
Continental	−0.164	−0.164	TWA	0.041	0.174
Delta	1.650	1.796	United	−1.395	−0.263
Eastern	−0.361	0.000	USAir	0.140	0.197
America West	−0.049	−0.051	Southwest	0.006	0.011

Source: Authors' calculations; see text.

shows, these findings are not particularly sensitive to parameter statistical precision or definition of market presence.

Although the lack of industry profitability, particularly the large losses in the 1990s, cannot be attributed to the pricing behavior of bankrupt carriers, individual carriers have been affected by bankruptcies in very different ways (table 5-4). United Airlines has lost an estimated $1.4 billion in revenue, while Delta has gained $1.7 billion. American Airlines, which has probably been most vocal in calling for changes in the laws to prevent carriers from remaining in bankruptcy indefinitely, has lost $220 million in revenue but only $43 million since 1989. Table 5-5 decomposes these totals by bankruptcy.

Why have United and to a lesser extent American been hurt by bankruptcies while Delta has prospered? The coefficients in table 5-6 indicate that the presence of a bankrupt carrier allowed Delta to increase fares in some markets from which it derived a large proportion of its revenue where it had substantial contact with such a carrier (for example, Eastern Airlines—Delta held a widely acknowledged superior reputation—Continental, and TWA). The opposite effect was found for American in the TWA bankruptcy and for United in the TWA and first Continental bankruptcy; apparently American and United could not exploit their better reputations in competition with these bankrupt carriers. It should not be surprising, then, that American and United have been more vocal than Delta in demanding changes in the laws that would reduce the time a carrier can spend in bankruptcy.

Table 5-5. *Estimated Effect of Bankrupt Airlines, by Occurrence,
on Revenue of Three Healthy Airlines*
Billions of dollars

Bankruptcy	Airline		
	American	Delta	United
Continental(1), September 1983–September 1986	−0.177	−0.146	−1.132
Eastern, March 1989–January 1991[a]	0.034	0.675	−0.149
Braniff(2), September 1989–November 1989[a]	−0.007	0.000	−0.010
Continental(2), December 1990–April 1993[b]	0.266	0.640	0.361
Pan American, January 1991–December 1991[a]	−0.110	−0.009	−0.161
Midway, March 1991–November 1991[a]	−0.008	−0.002	−0.042
America West, June 1991–August 1994[b]	0.250	0.144	0.283
TWA, February 1992–November 1993[b]	−0.469	0.347	−0.546
Total	−0.220	1.650	−1.395
Total since 1989	−0.043	1.796	−0.263

Source: Authors' calculations; see text.
a. Bankruptcy ended with liquidation.
b. Bankruptcy ended after the last period included in this analysis (third quarter 1992).

Multimarket Contact

Economists have long been concerned that companies can engage in
extensive cooperation and tacit collusion to raise prices if they encounter
each other in many markets.[41] This potential problem is clearly relevant
to the airline industry because some carriers share many routes. To the
extent that a large part of a carrier's revenue is earned in markets in
which it repeatedly competes with another carrier, both carriers have
strong financial incentives to engage in tacit collusion and avoid fare wars.
Multimarket contact could also make it easier for them to monitor each
other's fares and to detect deviations that are especially directed toward
them. However, tacit collusion—to the extent it exists—may break down
in hard economic times, which could lead to price wars as each carrier
competes fiercely for every passenger.[42] We are thus interested in multimarket contacts from the perspective of their implications for the industry's recent financial performance.

41. The matter was first raised by Corwin D. Edwards, "Conglomerate Bigness as a
Source of Power," in *Business Concentration and Price Policy: A Conference of the Univer-
sities–National Bureau for Economic Research* (Princeton University Press, 1955), pp. 331–
60. A recent theoretical treatment is by B. Douglas Bernheim and Michael D. Whinston,
"Multimarket Contact and Collusive Behavior," *Rand Journal of Economics*, vol. 21 (Spring
1990), pp. 1–26.
42. See F. M. Scherer, *Industrial Market Structure and Economic Performance*, 2d ed.
(Chicago: Rand-McNally, 1980).

Table 5-6.   *Estimated Effect of Bankrupt Airline on Fares of Three Healthy Airlines and Share of Healthy Airlines' Revenue in Markets Where They Compete with Bankrupt Airlines*

	Regression coefficient			Percent of revenue earned in market where carrier competes against bankrupt carrier		
Bankrupt carrier	American	Delta	United	American	Delta	United
Continental(1), September 1983–September 1986	−0.0512*	−0.0943*	−0.1940*	26.2	12.4	36.7
Eastern, March 1989– January 1991[a]	0.0197	0.1327*	−0.1007*	12.7	42.8	11.8
Braniff(2), September 1989– November 1989[a]	−1.0554*	. . .	−0.9226*	0.2	0.0	0.4
Continental(2), December 1990–April 1993[b]	0.0346	0.0855*	0.0480*	46.0	47.1	55.4
Pan American, January 1991–December 1991[a]	−0.0831*	−0.0132	−0.2373*	15.2	8.4	8.7
Midway, March 1991– November 1991[b]	−0.0342	−0.0113	−0.4353*	3.7	2.9	1.5
America West, June 1991– August 1994[b]	0.0734**	0.0714*	0.0838*	27.5	16.6	33.8
TWA, February 1991– November 1991[b]	−0.1164*	0.1273*	−0.1615*	43.8	34.1	44.6

Source: Authors' calculations; see text.
a. Bankruptcy ended with liquidation.
b. Bankruptcy ended after the last period included in this analysis (third quarter 1992).
*Significant at 5 percent level.
**Significant at 10 percent level.

Drawing on previous analyses, we estimated a fare equation for each carrier, but for this application the equation's distinctive feature was that it identified the effect of additional market contact with a given carrier on a carrier's fares, holding other influences constant.[43] As before, the background influences were route distance, route and airport concentration, route traffic density, and carrier contact dummies. Multimarket contact was measured carrier by carrier, leading to as many as fourteen contact variables in each carrier's fare equation. In particular, our measure of multimarket contact was the percentage of a carrier's revenue in

43. Bernheim and Whinston, "Multimarket Contact and Collusive Behavior," survey empirical investigations of multimarket contact in other industries. Previous studies of multimarket contact in the airline industry include William N. Evans and Ioannis N. Kessides, "Living by the 'Golden Rule': Multimarket Contact in the U.S. Airline Industry," *Quarterly Journal of Economics*, vol. 109 (May 1994), pp. 341–66; and Philippe Barla, "Multimarket Contact and Pricing Strategy in the U.S. Domestic Airline Sector," Department of Economics working paper, Cornell University, October 1993.

the 1,000 most heavily traveled routes that it earned in markets where it competed with a particular carrier. For example, in the third quarter of 1992 American earned 59 percent of its revenue in markets in which it competed with United, up from 40 percent in the fourth quarter of 1978.

Fares were estimated separately for all major carriers from the fourth quarter of 1978 to the third quarter of 1992, with the effect of multimarket contact therefore varying by carrier and year. Final estimations reflected the results of statistical tests, which did not reject the hypothesis of parameter stability, from the fourth quarter of 1978 to 1984, 1985 to 1990, and 1991 to the third quarter of 1992. (Estimation results for key parameters are presented in table 5A-3 in the appendix to this chapter.)[44] Based on these fare estimations, estimates of the industrywide effect of multimarket contact on fares are shown in figure 5-2.[45] (To be sure, as pointed out in chapter 2, deregulation has naturally led to more multimarket contact because it has led to more competition in city-pair combinations; what the figure shows, however, is the effect of this contact.) Multimarket contact does have an effect on fares in the industry, but changes seem highly sensitive to cyclical influences.[46] During the first few years of

44. We ran fifteen regressions, one for each carrier (the ten largest carriers in 1993, plus five others that had operated in bankruptcy and later exited the industry). For each regression the dependent variable was the log of that carrier's average fare for each of the top 1,000 routes it served. The independent variables were fifty-six quarterly time period dummy variables for each of the periods from the fourth quarter of 1978 to the third quarter of 1992, as many as fourteen carrier contact dummies (depending on the number of carriers that the carrier had some contact with), as many as eight bankruptcy contact dummies, as many as fourteen multimarket contact variables for each time period from the fourth quarter of 1978 to 1984, 1985 to 1990, and 1991 to the third quarter of 1992, and four variables in logs measuring distance, number of route passengers, number of effective competitors on the route, and the minimum number of effective competitors at the two airports that define the route.

45. Because our dependent variable is the log of average fare, the percentage by which contact with carrier B affects carrier A's fares (compared with no contact and relative to current fares) is given by $1 - \exp(-COEF \cdot MMVAR)$, where $MMVAR$ is the multimarket contact variable and $COEF$ is its regression coefficient. Because $MMVAR$ is the percentage of revenue that carrier A earns (on the top 1,000 routes) on routes on which it has contact with carrier B, multiplying the expression above by $MMVAR$ times carrier A's domestic passenger revenue gives an estimate of the effect of contact with carrier B on carrier A's revenue. These figures were calculated for all carriers used in the estimation procedure, the results were summed, and the result was divided by those carriers' aggregate domestic passenger revenue to obtain the aggregate results presented in the figure. In effect, the aggregate figure results from weighting the individual effects by the amount of contact and revenue involved.

46. As figure 5A-1 in the appendix to this chapter shows, the findings were surprisingly insensitive to assumptions as to which parameters were used in the calculations based on

Figure 5-2.   *Change in Airline Industry Average Fares Caused by Multimarket Contacts, 1979–92*

Percent

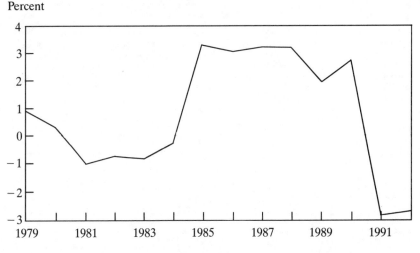

Source: Authors' calculations; see text.

deregulation, which coincided with slow economic growth, multimarket contact, as compared with no contact, did not lead to higher fares. But as the industry began to adjust to full deregulation in the second half of the 1980s and the economy grew more rapidly, multimarket contact increased fares by 2 to 3 percent and expanded industry revenue by $1 billion a year. Finally, from 1990 to 1992, years that witnessed a recession and an industry with more common multimarket contacts than in the early 1980s recession, carrier rivalry was intense and the resultant fare wars that erupted as carriers grimly tried to fill seats reduced fares 3 percent, which cut revenues by about $1.2 billion a year and contributed to the industry's financial crisis.[47]

---

their statistical precision. In the figure in the text, we used all the estimated multimarket parameter coefficients regardless of their statistical significance and, as before, defined a carrier as having a market presence if it carries more than 100 sampled passengers a quarter.

47. Using data from the fourth quarters of 1984 and 1988 and a somewhat different definition of multimarket contact, Evans and Kessides, "Living by the 'Golden Rule,'" concluded that fares in 1988 were 4 percent higher than fares in 1984 because of increases in multimarket contact. Our results are consistent with their finding. However, as is clear from the graph, 1984–88 turns out to be the period with the greatest effect of multimarket contact on fare elevation and is not representative of multimarket contact's effects over the business cycle.

Table 5-7. *Effect of Individual Multimarket Contact on Airline Revenue, by Airline, 1992*
Billions of dollars

Carriers affecting	Carriers affected							
	American	Alaska	Braniff[a]	Continental	Delta	Eastern[a]	America West	Midway[a]
American	...	−0.023	...	0.098	−0.821	...	0.002	...
Alaska	0.012	...	...	−0.001	0.023	...	−0.002	...
Braniff	...	...	...	...	...	...	...	...
Continental	−0.170	0.068	...	...	1.279	...	0.134	...
Delta	0.114	0.035	...	0.006	...	...	−0.001	...
Eastern	...	...	...	...	...	...	...	...
America West	−0.044	−0.082	...	−0.227	0.362	...	...	...
Midway	...	...	...	...	...	...	...	...
Northwest	−0.108	−0.026	...	0.077	0.008	...	0.009	...
Pan American	...	...	...	...	...	...	...	...
Air Florida	...	...	...	...	...	...	...	...
TWA	0.039	0.013	...	0.021	0.567	...	−0.064	...
United	1.410	0.156	...	−0.137	0.268	...	0.093	...
USAir	0.090	0.013	...	0.326	−0.364	...	−0.006	...
Southwest	−0.029	0	...	0.014	−0.017	...	0.134	...
Total	1.315	0.154	...	0.177	1.304	...	0.298	...

Table 5-7 shows the effect of multimarket contact on each carrier during 1992 (an entry of zero indicates absence of contact). Although the industry lost $1.17 billion in revenue from multimarket contact in 1992, American and Delta gained an estimated $1.3 billion each from contact. United, however, lost $2.8 billion and TWA $0.7 billion. These results suggest that as a carrier increased its contact with American, for instance, American was confident it could raise fares and the other carrier would go along. This result is consistent with the causality findings in chapter 4, which indicated American was the industry fare leader. Delta too appeared to be becoming an industry fare leader. But United's troubled competitive interactions, revealed in bankruptcy findings, surfaced once again. As a carrier, especially Continental or TWA, increased its contact with United, United was compelled to lower fares. American has been the prime beneficiary from multimarket contact since deregulation, and United the prime loser (table 5-8). Although Delta initially lost revenue, it has apparently been able to reverse its fortunes so that its benefits from multimarket contact now equal American's.

In general, the bankruptcy and multimarket contact findings suggest that a carrier can develop a reputation that discourages price-slashing

Carriers affecting		Carriers affected						
	Northwest	Pan American[a]	Air Florida[a]	TWA	United	USAir	Southwest	Total
American	−0.176	. . .	. . .	−0.427	−0.038	−0.075	0.004	−1.457
Alaska	0	. . .	. . .	−0.003	0.076	0.020	0	0.127
Braniff	. . .	. . .	. . .					
Continental	0.151	. . .	. . .	0.236	−1.516	0.009	0.010	0.202
Delta	−0.096	. . .	. . .	0.050	0.032	−0.462	0.018	−0.303
Eastern	. . .	. . .	. . .				. . .	. . .
America West	−0.032	. . .	. . .	−0.712	0.468	0.127	−0.026	−0.167
Midway	. . .	. . .	. . .		. . .		. . .	. . .
Northwest	. . .	. . .	. . .	−0.005	−0.537	−0.008	−0.007	−0.597
Pan American	. . .	. . .	. . .	. . .	. . .	. . .	. . .	. . .
Air Florida	. . .	. . .	. . .	. . .	. . .	. . .	. . .	. . .
TWA	−0.022	. . .	. . .	. . .	−1.361	−0.001	−0.002	−0.811
United	−0.213	. . .	. . .	0.200	. . .	−0.136	−0.021	1.620
USAir	0.107	. . .	. . .	−0.036	0.094	. . .	−0.007	0.216
Southwest	−0.036	. . .	. . .	−0.014	−0.009	−0.040	. . .	0.003
Total	−0.316	. . .	. . .	−0.711	−2.791	−0.567	−0.032	−1.169

Source: Authors' calculations; see text.
a. Carrier bankrupt and assets liquidated before 1992.

behavior by its competitors. It is of course an open question as to how American and Delta developed such interactions while United did not.

Conclusion

Financial success in the airline industry appears to stem from a combination of factors, few of which, with the possible exception of owning a computer reservation system, have anything to do with size. Low-cost operations, an efficient network, and an experienced business-educated management can be developed, in principle, by any airline.

The recent large losses cannot be attributed primarily to structural problems in the industry. The industry is more profitable in a deregulated environment than it was in a regulated one, and its revenues have not been significantly reduced by bankrupt carriers. Multimarket contact can either reduce or increase industry revenues, depending on cyclical influences, but not substantially. The primary source of carriers' losses appears to be their failure, because of poor forecasts, to adapt efficiently to changes in the business cycle and to the disruptions of the Persian Gulf

Table 5-8.   *Effect of All Multimarket Contact on Airline Revenue,*
by Airline, 1979–92
Billions of dollars

Year	American	Alaska	Braniff[a]	Continental	Delta	Eastern[b]	America West	Midway
1979	0.350	0.025	−0.022	0.026	−0.158	−0.107	. . .	0
1980	0.261	0.027	−0.013	0.034	−0.130	−0.116	. . .	0
1981	0.388	0.021	−0.027	0.017	−0.166	−0.228	. . .	−0.001
1982	0.591	0.017	−0.010	0.038	−0.221	−0.272	. . .	−0.001
1983	0.823	0.018	. . .	0.038	−0.328	−0.350	0.001	−0.074
1984	0.765	0.039	0.010	0.047	−0.400	−0.397	0.029	−0.007
1985	0.747	0.033	0.038	0.126	0.110	−0.085	0.032	0
1986	0.754	0.055	0.020	0.140	0.136	−0.082	0.050	−0.001
1987	0.753	0.049	0.026	0.242	0.277	0.016	0.046	−0.014
1988	0.973	0.117	0.043	0.274	0.205	0.073	0.002	0.012
1989	0.869	0.111	0.029	0.307	0.131	0.084	−0.020	0.014
1990	1.235	0.165	. . .	0.293	0.205	−0.001	−0.114	−0.050
1991	0.650	0.162	. . .	0.154	1.139	. . .	0.268	−0.025
1992	1.315	0.154	. . .	0.177	1.304	. . .	0.298	. . .

War and its impact on air travel and fuel prices. The resulting over-capacity forced most fares and revenues down.

The future of competition in the airline industry rests on management's ability to learn from this difficult period and to cope effectively with other contingencies that cannot be foreseen. From this view the extraordinary losses suffered by airlines in the past few years are as clear a message as a market is ever likely to send.

Appendix

This appendix presents the key estimation results and sensitivity tests of the effect on fares of competition with bankrupt carriers and multimarket contact. It also includes the derivation of the effect of fare changes on profits and the resulting adjustment factors that can be used to convert our findings on changes in revenue to changes in profits.

The Effect of Bankruptcy on Carrier Fares

Table 5A-1 presents the parameter estimates of the effect that each carrier bankruptcy had on the fares of the other carriers. The effect of each bankruptcy on industry and carrier revenue for the base case was shown in table 5-3. Table 5A-2 presents the results of the base case in

Year	Northwest	Pan American[c]	Air Florida[d]	TWA	United	USAir	Southwest	Total
1979	−0.008	0.016	−0.041	0.132	−0.091	0.015	0	0.137
1980	−0.001	0.081	−0.057	0.085	−0.148	0.020	0	0.044
1981	−0.027	0.067	−0.091	0.099	−0.261	0.001	0.001	−0.206
1982	−0.035	0.090	−0.088	0.063	−0.317	−0.007	0.001	−0.150
1983	−0.043	0.122	−0.060	0.094	−0.375	−0.046	0.003	−0.178
1984	−0.012	0.083	...	0.113	−0.267	−0.079	0.007	−0.067
1985	0.036	0.098	...	0.138	−0.422	−0.039	0	0.813
1986	0.037	0.126	...	0.165	−0.568	−0.043	0.002	0.790
1987	0.110	0.123	...	0.172	−0.730	−0.023	0.014	1.061
1988	0.096	0.172	...	0.209	−0.986	−0.024	0.020	1.186
1989	0.102	0.156	...	0.159	−1.061	−0.111	0.011	0.781
1990	0.134	0.088	...	0.022	−0.605	−0.196	0.021	1.196
1991	−0.270	−0.033	...	−0.595	−2.210	−0.446	−0.007	−1.212
1992	−0.316	...	...	−0.711	−2.791	−0.567	−0.032	−1.169

Source: Authors' calculations; see text.
a. Liquidated November 1989.
b. Liquidated January 1991.
c. Liquidated December 1991.
d. Liquidated July 1984.

the first column of figures, which used all the bankruptcy coefficient estimates, regardless of statistical significance (confidence level equals 100 percent), and included markets with at least one hundred sampled passengers per quarter (Q > 100). Results for alternative assumptions regarding market definition and admissible parameters according to statistical significance are also presented in the table. For example, Q > 0 includes markets with a least one sampled passenger per quarter, while a 1 percent confidence level means that we only used estimated coefficients that were statistically significant at the 1 percent level. The primary findings are not particularly sensitive to the choice of parameter statistical precision, or definition of market presence.

The Effect of Multimarket Contact on Fares

Table 5A-3 shows the parameter estimates of the effect that contact with a particular carrier during a given time period had on the fares of each of the other carriers. Figure 5-2 showed the effect of multimarket contact on fares using all the estimated multimarket parameter coefficients regardless of their statistical significance. Figure 5A-1 shows this

Table 5A-1. *Bankruptcy Regression Coefficients, by Carrier*[a]

Bankrupt carrier	American	Alaska	Continental	Delta	Eastern	America West	Midway
Braniff(2)	−1.055	...	...	...	...	...	...
	(0.031)						
Continental(1)	−0.051	−0.260	...	−0.094	−0.247	0.150	...
	(0.024)	(0.083)		(0.027)	(0.025)	(0.054)	
Continental(2)	0.035	−0.094	...	0.086	...	−0.031	...
	(0.025)	(0.094)		(0.021)		(0.043)	
Eastern	0.020	0.388	−0.017	0.133	...	...	−0.100
	(0.037)	(0.079)	(0.031)	(0.016)			(0.129)
America West	0.073	0.097	−0.086	0.071	...	...	...
	(0.044)	(0.062)	(0.043)	(0.035)			
Midway	−0.034	...	...	−0.011	...	...	...
	(0.060)			(0.028)			
Pan American	−0.083	−0.065	−0.105	−0.013	...	...	...
	(0.034)	(0.330)	(0.051)	(0.045)			
TWA	−0.116	0.300	−0.033	0.127	...	−0.067	...
	(0.042)	(0.129)	(0.040)	(0.024)		(0.052)	
Number of observations	9,434	1,205	6,398	10,860	8,443	1,855	868
$\bar{R}^2$	0.748	0.811	0.809	0.773	0.793	0.844	0.732

effect using alternative assumptions regarding admissible parameters according to statistical significance. Again, a 1 percent significance level, for example, means that we used only multimarket parameter coefficients that were statistically significant at the 1 percent level. The figure shows that the basic findings are not particularly sensitive to alternative assumptions regarding statistical precision.

Derivation of the Effect of a Price Change on Profits

Profits (Π) are defined as revenue (R) minus cost (C). Because we used accounting profits rather than economic profits in this chapter, cost—and thus profits—are defined in accounting terms rather than in economic terms.

The total differential of profits is $d\Pi = dR - dC$. Given that $R = Q(P)P$ and $C = C[Q(P)]$, where $Q(P)$ is quantity demanded and P is price, we have, after some manipulation,

$$dR = (1 - \eta) R \frac{dP}{P} \text{ and } dC = -\theta\eta C \frac{dP}{P},$$

where η is the absolute value of the price elasticity of demand ($-dQ/dP \cdot P/Q$) and θ is the cost elasticity ($dC/dQ \cdot Q/C$).

Bankrupt carrier	Northwest	Pan American	TWA	United	USAir	Southwest
Braniff(2)	...	...	−0.949	−0.923	...	...
			(0.038)	(0.026)		
Continental(1)	−0.100	−0.108	−0.109	−0.194	−0.378	−0.049
	(0.024)	(0.029)	(0.041)	(0.013)	(0.060)	(0.028)
Continental(2)	0.020	0.018	0.133	0.048	0.134	−0.022
	(0.028)	(0.053)	(0.038)	(0.014)	(0.024)	(0.027)
Eastern	0.035	−0.077	0.085	−0.101	−0.059	...
	(0.045)	(0.044)	(0.035)	(0.037)	(0.029)	
America West	−0.004	...	−0.042	0.084	0.101	0.028
	(0.099)		(0.061)	(0.036)	(0.033)	(0.017)
Midway	−0.029	...	...	−0.435	−0.039	−0.080
	(0.153)			(0.042)	(0.046)	(0.075)
Pan American	−0.085	...	−0.133	−0.237	−0.255	...
	(0.063)		(0.049)	(0.061)	(0.044)	
TWA	−0.059	...	...	−0.161	−0.114	0.006
	(0.062)			(0.031)	(0.038)	(0.032)
Number of observations	5,584	1,913	5,711	10,921	8,027	4,395
$\bar{R}^2$	0.767	0.820	0.808	0.779	0.757	0.881

Source: Authors' calculations; see text.

a. Columns show bankruptcy regression coefficients from one regression: the fares of the carrier in the column heading were regressed on the bankruptcy dummy for the carrier shown in the stub, plus other control variables. White heteroskedastic standard errors are in parentheses.

If we use M to indicate the gross margin, $(R - C)/R$, we can express C as $R(1 - M)$. Combining terms we have

$$d\Pi = [1 - \eta + (1 - M)\theta\eta] \, R \, \frac{dP}{P},$$

which expresses the change in accounting profit as a function of the demand and cost elasticities, revenue, the margin, and the percentage change in price. Given its derivation, this formula only holds for very small changes in price. However, it provides a useful approximation for our purposes. Given that the last two terms in the equation above, $R \, (dP/P)$, equal the change in revenue assuming no demand response (and thus no change in cost) as we assume in the tables in the text, we can approximate the change in profits by multiplying the figures in tables 5-3, 5-4, 5-7, 5-8, and 5A-2 by $1 - \eta + (1 - M) \, \theta\eta$.

Two rules of thumb in the industry are that $\eta = 0.7$ and $\theta = 0.2$ in the short run when capacity is taken as given. Research on long-run industry costs usually finds constant returns to scale, implying $\theta = 1.0$ in the long run. A short-run perspective seems appropriate in the case of competing against bankrupt carriers because it seems unlikely that

Table 5A-2. *Effect of Bankruptcies on Airline Industry Profits*
Billions of dollars

	Confidence level = 100 percent			Confidence level = 1 percent		
Carrier	Q>100	Q>0	Q>200	Q>0	Q>100	Q>200
Bankrupt carrier						
Braniff 2	-0.018	-0.008	0	0.049	-0.018	0
Continental 1	-2.151	-2.070	-2.035	-1.972	-1.969	-1.766
Continental 2	1.942	2.837	1.348	2.195	1.659	1.114
Eastern	0.536	-0.112	0.878	0.143	0.539	0.933
America West	0.659	1.032	0.623	0.490	0.063	0.302
Midway	-0.068	-0.207	-0.022	-0.060	-0.042	-0.018
Air Florida	0	-0.010	0	-0.000	0	0
Pan American	-0.444	-1.325	-0.407	-1.026	-0.285	-0.188
TWA	-0.963	-1.358	-0.643	-0.728	-0.834	-0.579
Total	-0.508	-1.222	-0.257	-0.910	-0.887	-0.202
Total since 1989	1.643	0.858	1.778	1.062	1.082	1.564
Affected carrier						
American	-0.220	-0.664	-0.085	-0.335	-0.476	-0.333
Alaska	0.009	0.038	0.005	0.033	-0.009	0.028
Braniff	0	-0.030	0.011	0	0	0.012
Continental	-0.164	-0.251	-0.071	-0.188	0	0
Delta	1.650	1.090	1.343	0.889	1.517	1.314
Eastern	-0.361	-0.314	-0.307	-0.309	-0.361	-0.307
America West	-0.049	0.182	-0.003	0.149	0.002	0
Midway	-0.009	-0.051	0.017	-0.034	0	0
Northwest	-0.102	-0.117	0.031	-0.108	-0.088	-0.007
Pan American	-0.051	-0.079	-0.064	0	-0.032	-0.032
Air Florida	0	-0.001	0	-0.001	0	0
TWA	0.041	0.160	0.048	0.078	-0.016	0.222
United	-1.395	-1.581	-1.229	-1.793	-1.679	-1.200
USAir	0.140	0.543	0.046	0.708	0.255	0.105
Southwest	0.006	-0.148	0	0	0	-0.005
Affected carrier since 1989						
American	-0.043	-0.142	0.065	0.187	-0.476	-0.333
Alaska	0.030	0.075	0.020	0.033	0.012	0.044
Braniff	0	-0.010	0.012	0	0	0.012
Continental	-0.164	-0.251	-0.071	-0.188	0	0
Delta	1.796	1.306	1.448	1.105	1.663	1.420
Eastern	0	-0.002	0	0	0	0
America West	-0.051	0.172	-0.003	0.149	0	0
Midway	-0.009	-0.042	0.017	-0.034	0	0
Northwest	-0.014	-0.009	0.103	0	0	0.066
Pan Americn	-0.019	-0.036	-0.032	0	0	0
Air Florida	0	0	0	0	0	0
TWA	0.174	0.297	0.166	0.214	0.117	0.222
United	-0.263	-0.927	-0.038	-0.137	-0.547	-0.010
USAir	0.197	0.570	0.084	0.732	0.313	0.143
Southwest	0.011	-0.141	0.006	0	0	0

Source: Authors' calculations; see text.

Figure 5A-1. *Estimated Effects of Multimarket Contacts on Fares,*
1979–92

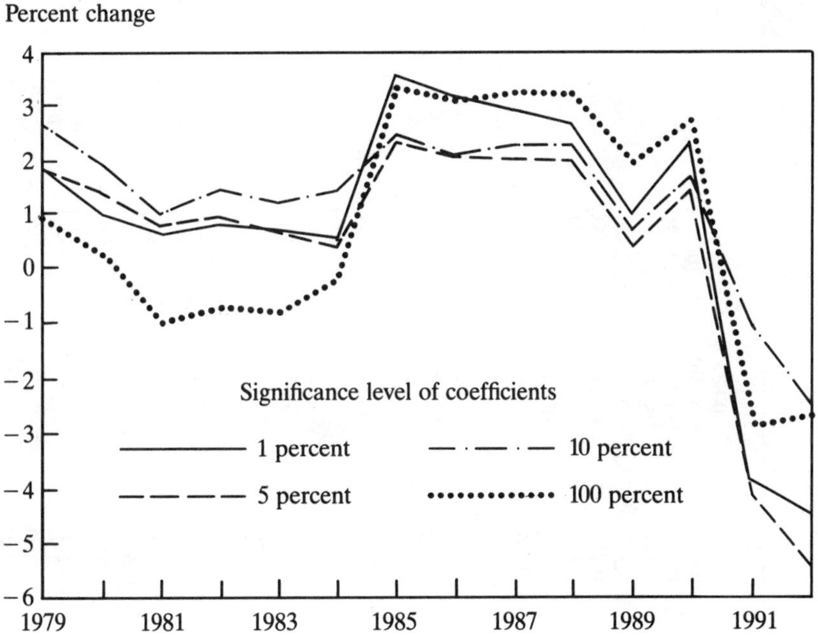

Percent change

Source: Authors' calculations; see text.

carriers would add capacity in this situation. A long-run perspective
seems appropriate in the multimarket case because of the protracted
nature of this effect. Given that the gross margin is close to zero even in
good years, the factor above equals approximately 0.44 in the short run
for the bankruptcy case and approximately 1.0 in the long run for the
multimarket contact case.

Table 5A-3. *Multimarket Contact Regression Coefficients, by Airline*[a]

Carrier	American	Alaska	Braniff	Continental	Delta	Eastern	America West	Midway
1978–84								
American	...	0.505	−0.173	0.244	−0.837	1.083	0.544	−2.099
		(2.178)	(0.060)	(0.073)	(0.156)	(0.227)	(0.442)	(1.105)
Alaska	−1333.762	...	25.630	50.019	−136.729	−99.721	...	...
	(176.874)		(58.825)	(16.743)	(45.888)	(90.278)		
Braniff	−0.810	2.891	...	0.348	−0.175	1.280	...	−50.210
	(0.291)	(1.542)		(0.215)	(0.276)	(0.253)		(18.590)
Continental	−0.007	5.658	−0.422	...	0.114	0.094	...	...
	(0.226)	(1.737)	(0.281)		(0.539)	(0.340)		
Delta	−0.140	1.992	0.246	−0.118	...	−0.257	−0.309	−3.273
	(0.139)	(1.142)	(0.080)	(0.149)		(0.077)	(0.652)	(1.421)
Eastern	−0.327	−5.136	−1.391	−0.218	−0.094	...	0.408	31.950
	(0.310)	(2.163)	(0.537)	(0.122)	(0.090)		(0.740)	(10.169)
America West	32.106	...	...	...	51.391	33.634	...	...
	(28.606)				(39.815)	(15.646)		
Midway	3.055	...	−0.978	...	19.058	65.056	...	...
	(2.345)		(3.993)		(7.416)	(18.195)		
Northwest	−0.209	0.259	1.091	−0.420	−0.394	0.393	−0.296	−1.143
	(0.168)	(0.116)	(0.846)	(0.452)	(0.229)	(0.394)	(0.854)	(0.637)
Pan American	0.001	1.088	2.114	0.544	0.699	0.289	...	...
	(0.391)	(0.389)	(0.738)	(0.223)	(0.329)	(0.124)		
Air Florida	−112.297	...	−2.753	−5.689	0.221	0.642	...	...
	(25.861)		(1.702)	(5.064)	(0.646)	(0.236)		
TWA	0.411	2.051	−1.368	0.453	0.813	−0.237	−0.421	...
	(0.213)	(2.741)	(0.610)	(0.264)	(0.262)	(0.119)	(0.299)	
United	0.723	0.512	0.455	−0.075	−0.108	−0.824	0.774	...
	(0.098)	(0.189)	(0.221)	(0.086)	(0.312)	(0.337)	(0.296)	
USAir	0.182	...	−5.402	−1.514	−1.372	−1.752	−0.294	−7.919
	(0.288)		(2.442)	(2.013)	(0.611)	(0.269)	(0.305)	(3.756)
Southwest	−26.004	...	−1.531	0.902	−0.418	−85.910	1.137	...
	(9.976)		(1.897)	(0.652)	(7.270)	(30.146)	(0.122)	

Carrier	Northwest	Pan American	Air Florida	TWA	United	USAir	Southwest
1978–84							
American	-0.385 (0.199)	-0.048 (0.128)	-1.221 (2.320)	-0.243 (0.166)	0.040 (0.052)	0.192 (0.468)	-0.500 (0.511)
Alaska	2.971 (1.629)	-19.750 (11.571)	⋯	-1038.236 (404.610)	3.609 (3.610)	⋯	⋯
Braniff	2.279 (0.849)	-0.381 (0.387)	0.138 (0.179)	0.893 (0.754)	0.300 (0.553)	4.172 (0.962)	3.459 (1.669)
Continental	0.043 (0.199)	-0.183 (0.179)	-1.649 (4.906)	-0.226 (0.218)	-0.195 (0.080)	-6.017 (2.731)	-0.719 (0.568)
Delta	-1.294 (0.406)	0.263 (0.115)	-0.212 (0.113)	0.310 (0.213)	-0.428 (0.182)	-0.885 (0.571)	1.726 (0.782)
Eastern	0.633 (0.279)	0.183 (0.093)	-0.622 (0.356)	-0.071 (0.129)	0.535 (0.211)	-0.690 (0.249)	-4.512 (1.649)
America West	105.539 (20.410)	⋯	⋯	-21.827 (7.336)	6.580 (18.979)	141.626 (76.141)	0.913 (0.410)
Midway	0.509 (1.085)	⋯	⋯			-29.413 (20.559)	⋯
Northwest	⋯	0.457 (0.214)	0.762 (0.821)	-0.513 (0.222)	-0.347 (0.096)	0.742 (0.488)	8.940 (2.810)
Pan American	0.493 (0.727)	⋯	0.468 (0.151)	0.503 (0.389)	-0.379 (0.448)	-1.119 (4.056)	2.045 (3.865)
Air Florida	6.173 (4.992)	-0.428 (0.257)	⋯	-2.653 (0.880)	10.371 (8.461)	0.713 (9.920)	⋯
TWA	-0.384 (0.527)	0.231 (0.125)	-0.369 (0.171)	⋯	-0.116 (0.159)	0.373 (0.138)	0.901 (0.623)
United	-0.094 (0.097)	0.038 (0.116)	-1.150 (0.654)	0.572 (0.141)	⋯	-0.064 (0.370)	1.596 (0.844)
USAir	0.342 (0.281)	7.095 (2.002)	0.987 (1.242)	-0.116 (0.174)	0.309 (0.210)	⋯	-2.954 (1.697)
Southwest	-51.112 (21.600)	12.862 (8.909)	⋯	-2.004 (5.002)	5.158 (2.674)	-12.830 (66.645)	⋯

Table 5A-3. (Continued)

Carrier	American	Alaska	Braniff	Continental	Delta	Eastern	America West	Midway
1985–90								
American	⋯	-0.064 (0.187)	0.035 (0.046)	0.154 (0.053)	-0.211 (0.055)	0.216 (0.069)	-0.004 (0.203)	-2.969 (1.019)
Alaska	1.905 (1.157)	⋯	-4.582 (60.183)	25.098 (6.987)	8.786 (2.855)	-13.496 (41.908)	-1.904 (0.650)	⋯
Braniff	-0.423 (0.288)	-63.633 (73.468)	⋯	0.135 (0.552)	0.020 (0.252)	0.064 (0.197)	-0.060 (1.756)	-21.684 (10.008)
Continental	-0.030 (0.081)	0.180 (0.276)	-0.172 (0.080)	⋯	0.277 (0.098)	0.029 (0.120)	-1.386 (0.357)	0.516 (0.244)
Delta	-0.028 (0.086)	0.130 (0.223)	0.382 (0.057)	0.111 (0.114)	⋯	-0.066 (0.071)	0.147 (0.190)	-1.005 (0.648)
Eastern	-0.408 (0.116)	2.519 (2.011)	-0.199 (0.087)	0.034 (0.090)	0.048 (0.089)	⋯	0.066 (0.386)	1.973 (0.893)
America West	0.169 (0.267)	-0.831 (0.378)	-0.449 (0.572)	-1.254 (0.425)	2.291 (0.527)	-6.059 (9.220)		-7.329 (4.256)
Midway	-0.103 (2.726)	⋯	-1.203 (1.314)	1.492 (2.325)	3.779 (1.438)	4.431 (2.627)	0.327 (2.289)	⋯
Northwest	-0.307 (0.100)	-0.248 (0.210)	0.340 (0.184)	0.184 (0.201)	-0.041 (0.137)	0.214 (0.192)	-0.429 (0.448)	0.046 (0.457)
Pan American	0.381 (0.344)	1.051 (0.768)	2.003 (0.489)	0.346 (0.612)	0.915 (0.550)	0.334 (0.134)	-2.932 (4.700)	30.333 (7.831)
Air Florida	⋯	⋯	⋯	⋯	⋯	⋯	⋯	⋯
TWA	0.172 (0.220)	0.866 (0.556)	0.020 (0.167)	0.003 (0.277)	0.224 (0.172)	-0.269 (0.112)	-0.862 (0.247)	7.479 (1.683)
United	0.659 (0.078)	0.479 (0.117)	0.122 (0.083)	-0.031 (0.083)	0.365 (0.102)	-0.138 (0.100)	0.706 (0.227)	-0.252 (0.843)
USAir	0.064 (0.090)	0.558 (0.211)	-0.649 (0.208)	0.537 (0.109)	-0.322 (0.082)	-0.088 (0.051)	0.033 (0.200)	-0.504 (0.209)
Southwest	-13.573 (6.008)	-22.488 (15.430)	-0.821 (0.395)	3.719 (0.603)	-0.445 (4.500)	-9.705 (2.577)	0.949 (0.122)	-0.447 (0.704)

Carrier	Northwest	Pan American	Air Florida	TWA	United	USAir	Southwest
1985–90							
American	-0.399	-0.190	...	-0.316	0.045	-0.045	-0.184
	(0.116)	(0.114)		(0.141)	(0.037)	(0.133)	(0.394)
Alaska	1.512	5.302	...	-4.916	2.942	1.766	0.718
	(1.312)	(5.477)		(8.392)	(1.302)	(0.782)	(2.750)
Braniff	0.630	-0.320	...	0.685	0.266	-0.106	1.618
	(0.361)	(0.526)		(0.425)	(0.319)	(2.385)	(1.574)
Continental	0.250	-0.657	...	-0.229	-0.215	0.335	0.223
	(0.092)	(0.242)		(0.112)	(0.045)	(0.250)	(0.113)
Delta	0.086	0.342	...	0.343	-0.011	-0.338	0.134
	(0.147)	(0.168)		(0.104)	(0.081)	(0.218)	(0.268)
Eastern	0.212	0.327	...	0.135	0.264	-0.119	-1.959
	(0.192)	(0.102)		(0.082)	(0.076)	(0.141)	(1.093)
America West	1.019	0.401	...	-2.402	1.495	4.079	0.112
	(0.889)	(1.156)		(0.676)	(0.301)	(1.003)	(0.179)
Midway	1.051	1.411	...	-5.316	-5.795	-0.196	4.620
	(0.382)	(0.563)		(4.144)	(4.195)	(0.347)	(1.814)
Northwest	...	0.183	...	0.195	-0.353	-0.087	-1.299
		(0.118)		(0.109)	(0.073)	(0.296)	(1.108)
Pan American	-0.667	...	...	0.426	0.158	-1.033	3.306
	(0.533)			(0.266)	(0.424)	(1.044)	(2.842)
Air Florida	...	...	...	...	...	...	...
TWA	0.337	0.300	...	...	-0.502	-0.102	-0.200
	(0.260)	(0.105)			(0.166)	(0.315)	(0.284)
United	-0.090	0.465	...	0.684	...	0.150	0.662
	(0.090)	(0.109)		(0.144)		(0.172)	(0.584)
USAir	0.356	0.252	...	0.236	0.227	...	-0.255
	(0.253)	(0.364)		(0.139)	(0.085)		(0.294)
Southwest	-0.717	-11.360	...	0.068	2.700	-7.404	...
	(1.047)	(34.931)		(0.404)	(2.016)	(1.869)	

Table 5A-3. *(Continued)*

Carrier	American	Alaska	Braniff	Continental	Delta	Eastern	America West	Midway
1991–92								
American	...	-0.157 (0.214)	...	0.073 (0.066)	-0.214 (0.050)	...	0.007 (0.139)	-2.086 (0.797)
Alaska	3.746 (2.889)	...	...	-27.614 (22.575)	6.884 (2.735)	...	-0.738 (1.823)	...
Braniff	...	...	...	...	...	...	...	...
Continental	-0.086 (0.370)	3.229 (1.742)	...	...	0.900 (0.484)	...	0.870 (1.421)	...
Delta	0.030 (0.070)	0.229 (0.198)	...	0.006 (0.103)	...	...	-0.004 (0.141)	-1.053 (0.759)
Eastern	...	...	...	...	...	...	...	...
America West	-0.065 (0.211)	-0.610 (0.436)	...	-1.476 (0.462)	1.551 (0.484)	...	...	...
Midway	-0.964 (1.861)	...	...	...	2.286 (1.059)	...	...	...
Northwest	-0.115 (0.105)	-0.570 (0.290)	...	0.327 (0.149)	0.013 (0.096)	...	0.163 (0.324)	0.338 (0.887)
Pan American	-2.919 (4.177)	24.844 (2.614)	...	-2.510 (2.668)	0.634 (1.387)	...	...	...
Air Florida	...	...	...	...	...	...	...	...
TWA	0.025 (0.292)	11.155 (2.686)	...	0.132 (0.374)	0.631 (0.176)	...	-0.666 (0.184)	...
United	0.585 (0.082)	0.448 (0.112)	...	-0.138 (0.088)	0.202 (0.091)	...	0.453 (0.169)	-0.817 (0.553)
USAir	0.136 (0.094)	0.553 (0.529)	...	0.720 (0.089)	-0.215 (0.060)	...	-0.114 (0.268)	-1.686 (0.630)
Southwest	-5.165 (4.771)	-58.021 (24.655)	...	3.954 (1.845)	-3.322 (4.367)	...	1.666 (0.161)	-0.243 (0.618)
Number of observations	9,434	1,205	2,088	6,398	10,860	8,443	1,855	868
$\bar{R}^2$	0.754	0.823	0.857	0.813	0.780	0.801	0.853	0.749

Carrier	Northwest	Pan American	Air Florida	TWA	United	USAIR	Southwest
1991–92							
American	-0.152 (0.090)	-0.339 (0.130)	...	-0.291 (0.126)	-0.011 (0.040)	-0.067 (0.117)	0.139 (0.440)
Alaska	0.413 (3.234)	-0.783 (19.625)	...	-18.010 (8.478)	2.464 (0.999)	7.918 (2.713)	0.503 (1.925)
Braniff	...	...	...	...	...	...	...
Continental	0.147 (0.322)	0.162 (0.327)	...	1.088 (0.576)	-0.565 (0.216)	0.012 (0.537)	1.066 (0.625)
Delta	-0.127 (0.115)	0.355 (0.109)	...	0.064 (0.071)	0.021 (0.074)	-0.357 (0.163)	0.469 (0.361)
Eastern	...	...	...	...		...	...
America West	-0.482 (0.894)	...	...	-2.523 (0.513)	0.677 (0.235)	4.008 (1.224)	-0.180 (0.191)
Midway	0.539 (1.111)	...	...	...	-12.825 (2.025)	-0.335 (0.676)	2.969 (2.177)
Northwest	...	0.137 (0.278)	...	-0.016 (0.140)	-0.380 (0.086)	-0.018 (0.198)	-3.603 (1.837)
Pan American	-2.145 (2.392)	...	...	-0.264 (1.440)	1.715 (2.168)	0.612 (2.025)	...
Air Florida	...	...	...	...	...	...	...
TWA	-0.038 (0.298)	0.132 (0.175)	...	...	-0.836 (0.197)	-0.003 (0.272)	-0.173 (0.356)
United	-0.270 (0.106)	-0.051 (0.187)	...	0.362 (0.144)	...	-0.387 (0.202)	-0.554 (0.336)
USAir	0.385 (0.183)	-0.387 (0.205)	...	-0.149 (0.123)	0.140 (0.091)	...	-0.746 (0.326)
Southwest	-1.901 (1.378)	...	...	-0.313 (0.409)	-1.477 (2.059)	-4.532 (2.282)	...
Number of observations	5,584	1,913	364	5,711	10,921	8,027	4,395
$\bar{R}^2$	0.774	0.831	0.853	0.814	0.785	0.765	0.885

Source: Authors' calculations; see text.

a. Each column in the table shows multimarket contact regression coefficients from one regression: the log of the fares of the carrier in column heading were regressed on the contact measure of the carriers and during the time periods given in the stub, plus other control variables. White heteroskedastic standard errors are in parentheses.

CHAPTER SIX

Industry Evolution

BECAUSE of the business cycle and the large income elasticity of demand for air travel, airline profits will always fluctuate. But will industry profits ever cycle around a normal return for a sustained period? Even more to the point, will they ever do so in any industry structure except one that consists of only a few carriers—with travelers paying much higher fares than they do now? This chapter identifies the factors that will shape the evolution of the airline industry and estimates the effects of possible industry shakeouts on both travelers and carriers.

Airline Fares and Market Entry and Exit

Airlines are constantly entering and exiting markets. When one carrier leaves the industry, others enter its markets. The effect of these changes on fares depends on the characteristics of the incumbent and new carriers. If a low-cost carrier leaves the industry and high-cost carriers take over its routes, fares will probably rise. If a high-cost carrier leaves the industry and low-cost carriers take over its routes, fares will probably fall. Carriers have different pricing policies and react differently to other carriers' policies. The causality findings in chapter 4 are a good example of this point. As figures 6-1 to 6-5 show, for example, although all carriers expanded during the mid-1980s and early 1990s, they also had different market entry and exit patterns. Since deregulation, Southwest and American have shown steady growth in routes served. USAir and Delta showed relatively steady growth in routes served until the mid-1980s, when both began rapid expansion, partly through merger (USAir's merger with Piedmont accounted for a large part of its spectacular expansion in late 1987; see figure 6-3). United has experienced a more obvious cyclical growth.

Our interest here is to discuss the effect on fares of the different industry structures that result when carriers exit the industry. We also

Figure 6-1.   *Connecting and Direct Routes Served, Southwest Airlines, 1979–93*[a]

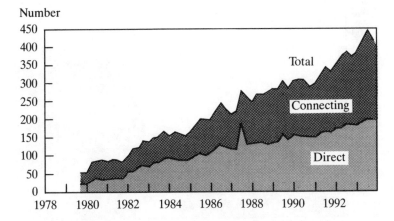

Source: Authors' calculations based on data in Department of Transportation Data Bank 1A. Routes served per quarter, both domestic and international, are the number of routes on which an airline carried more than one hundred sampled passengers per quarter (about one flight a week). If a carrier offered both direct and connecting service on a route, the service that carried more passengers was given credit.

a. Although Southwest was operating before the fourth quarter of 1979, it did not file the information with Data Bank 1A.

Figure 6-2.   *Connecting and Direct Routes Served, American Airlines, 1978–93*

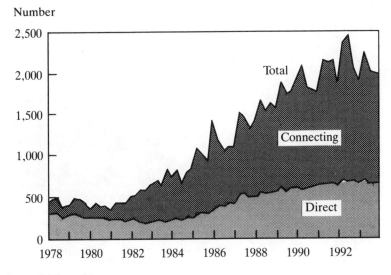

Source: See figure 6-1.

Figure 6-3. *Connecting and Direct Routes Served, USAir, 1978–93*[a]

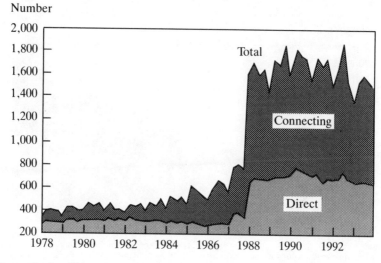

Source: See figure 6-1.
a. Sudden increase in routes served in 1987 was caused by absorption of Piedmont Airlines.

Figure 6-4. *Connecting and Direct Routes Served, Delta Airlines,
1978–93*

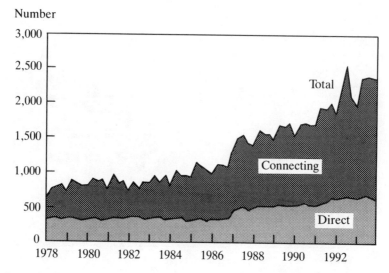

Source: See figure 6-1.

Figure 6-5. *Connecting and Direct Routes Served, United Airlines, 1978–93*

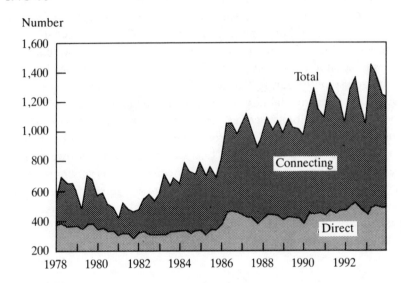

Source: See figure 6-1.

wanted to account for the remaining carriers' market entries and exits in response to a change in structure. We therefore needed to estimate models that measured the effect a carrier's exit from the industry would have on each remaining carrier's fares, entry, and exit in specific markets. Ideally, these models would be derived from a behavioral structural model of the airline industry. But developing such a model is difficult because individual airlines seem to follow very different behavioral patterns, even within their own network. Peter C. Reiss and Pablo T. Spiller and Steven T. Berry have developed and applied entry models to specialized air transport markets, but we were not able to generalize either of their models to analyze pricing, entry, and exit behavior for the entire industry.[1]

We therefore took a simpler approach and directly estimated fare, entry, and exit equations for each airline and used the equations to analyze the consequences of different industry structures. We assumed

1. Peter C. Reiss and Pablo T. Spiller, "Competition and Entry in Small Airline Markets," *Journal of Law and Economics*, vol. 32, pt. 2 (October 1989), pp. 179–202, studied entry behavior in small airline markets with at most one firm offering direct service. Steven T. Berry, "Estimation of a Model of Entry in the Airline Industry," *Econometrica*, vol. 60 (July 1992), pp. 889–917, was forced to assume for purposes of empirical tractability that a carrier made independent entry decisions on each route.

that the parameters for these equations remain unchanged as industry structures are altered. This assumption is plausible for the more realistic possibilities, which involve a small number of exits instead of massive restructuring. In addition, because we were interested in simulating the evolution of the airline industry during the next few years, we confined our estimation to the recent past, 1988–92. We did not statistically reject parameter stability during this period, but we did find in exploratory work that structural stability was not maintained much further back in time.[2] All specifications were estimated with quarterly data on airlines' conduct for direct flights at the route level (based on the most heavily traveled 1,000 routes in 1990) for 1988–92.[3] In all variations we present results for our base case, in which, to be considered as serving a route, an airline had to carry at least 600 sampled passengers a quarter, about one flight a day given that we were using a 10 percent sample. The sensitivity of our simulation results to different assumptions is given in the appendix to this chapter.

Fares

In our model, each carrier's fare was determined with a fare equation. But as in previous applications of this equation, its specification had to be tailored to the problem at hand. The key feature of the equation is that it specifies dummy variables indicating whether a particular carrier serves a route. Given our interest in the interaction between entry and exit behavior and airline fares, these dummy variables were used to capture the effect that a particular carrier's market presence has on another carrier's fare. Unlike the baseline model, we did not hold the number of effective competitors in the market (or at an airport) constant because we were interested in the effect on fares of removing a particular carrier from a route, not of removing a particular carrier and replacing it with the average carrier. Thus the coefficient of a carrier's presence dummy in another carrier's fare equation indicates how the other carrier's fares would differ on two routes that would be identical except for the presence of the carrier in question. If airlines were identical (same market

2. Steven A. Morrison and Clifford Winston, "The Dynamics of Airline Pricing and Competition," *American Economic Review*, vol. 80 (May 1990), pp. 389–93, reported, for example, estimates of entry models that showed a structural shift from partial deregulation in 1979–82 to full deregulation beginning in 1983.

3. The data used in this chapter are from Department of Transportation Data Bank 1A.

niche, strategy, and so forth) we expected the signs of the coefficients of the dummy variables to be negative; fares fall when another carrier enters a market. If, however, carriers and interactions differ, positive signs are possible and can be thought of as an indication, for example, that a given carrier's presence in a market provides an umbrella for other carriers to raise fares. As in other fare equations, we included route distance and the population at the origin and destination metropolitan areas (to control for traffic density). Finally, we included a variable that indicates the presence, either at the origin or destination, of an airport where flight operations are limited. (This additional variable was also relevant for entry and exit behavior.) These so-called slot-controlled airports— Chicago O'Hare, Washington National, and New York Kennedy and LaGuardia—effectively reduce competition and could therefore partly explain the variation of fares across routes. (Policy alternatives to slot-controlled airports are discussed in chapter 7.)

Table 6-1 presents estimates of the carrier dummy variables (estimates of the full model are contained in appendix table 6A-1) and shows a broad range of effects.[4] At one extreme the presence of Southwest, the industry's premier low-cost carrier, reduces the fare of every carrier it competes with (see the last column of table 6-1). The presence of America West and American does, too, but not so much. Because American is not a low-cost carrier, its effect on other carriers probably stems from its aggressive behavior, which might tend to provoke fare wars. At the other extreme the presence of United, a high-cost carrier, raises more carriers' fares than it lowers. The presence of the remaining carriers lowers more carriers' fares than it raises. Regardless of these systematic variations, a given carrier usually responds to the presence of other carriers by lowering its fares. Exceptions are America West and Alaska Air, whose responses are mixed.

Entry to Routes

To evaluate the determinants of a carrier's decision to provide direct service in a market, we estimated a probit model of entry behavior. For a given quarter, carriers were assumed to have the opportunity to enter any sampled market receiving airline service that they did not serve in the previous quarter. In general, market entry, like fares, is influenced

4. As a check for endogeneity, we instrumented the carrier dummy variables using a reduced-form probit model to predict the probability of entry (see below). The difference between the resulting parameter estimates and those in the table was negligible.

Table 6-1. Estimated Effects on an Airline's Fare of the Presence of Another Airline on a Given Route[a]

Carrier	Carrier presence dummy variables									
	American	Alaska	Continental	Delta	America West	Northwest	TWA	United	USAir	Southwest
American	· · ·	0.054	-0.192	-0.072	-0.227	-0.162	-0.170	0.001	-0.046	-0.350
		(0.031)	(0.021)	(0.014)	(0.019)	(0.029)	(0.038)	(0.019)	(0.019)	(0.072)
Alaska	-0.037	· · ·	-0.201	0.084	-0.183	0.047	0.160	0.079	0.026	-1.052
	(0.034)		(0.058)	(0.030)	(0.028)	(0.037)	(0.198)	(0.026)	(0.031)	(0.096)
Continental	-0.210	-0.180	· · ·	-0.022	-0.188	-0.076	-0.159	0.118	0.064	-0.315
	(0.021)	(0.056)		(0.017)	(0.023)	(0.023)	(0.029)	(0.010)	(0.017)	(0.034)
Delta	-0.209	-0.164	-0.079	· · ·	-0.133	-0.085	-0.156	0.040	-0.231	-0.740
	(0.014)	(0.033)	(0.018)		(0.024)	(0.017)	(0.022)	(0.017)	(0.014)	(0.062)
America West	-0.053	0.191	0.018	0.071	· · ·	0.023	0.021	0.107	-0.047	-0.404
	(0.021)	(0.034)	(0.029)	(0.020)		(0.038)	(0.033)	(0.029)	(0.019)	(0.014)
Northwest	-0.108	-0.168	-0.030	-0.109	-0.210	· · ·	-0.178	-0.014	-0.115	-0.625
	(0.028)	(0.032)	(0.021)	(0.016)	(0.027)		(0.033)	(0.019)	(0.023)	(0.067)
TWA	-0.044	-0.606	-0.095	-0.248	-0.169	-0.103	· · ·	-0.056	-0.146	-0.495
	(0.030)	(0.051)	(0.034)	(0.027)	(0.045)	(0.047)		(0.026)	(0.041)	(0.028)
United	-0.008	0.094	0.061	-0.037	-0.184	-0.092	-0.065	· · ·	-0.122	-0.713
	(0.012)	(0.023)	(0.009)	(0.012)	(0.019)	(0.018)	(0.029)		(0.018)	(0.031)
USAir	-0.138	-0.127	-0.008	-0.145	-0.381	0.052	-0.033	-0.237	· · ·	-0.628
	(0.019)	(0.037)	(0.014)	(0.014)	(0.023)	(0.021)	(0.027)	(0.018)		(0.026)
Southwest	-0.068	-0.063	0.123	-0.034	-0.248	-0.145	-0.095	-0.178	-0.117	· · ·
	(0.062)	(0.081)	(0.030)	(0.029)	(0.013)	(0.036)	(0.016)	(0.026)	(0.023)	

Source: Authors' calculations; see text.
a. Heteroskedastic-consistent standard errors in parentheses. Dependent variable is log real fare.

by the competition on the route and characteristics of the route, especially the way it is integrated with the carrier's and its competitors' networks.

As with the fare equation, the presence of other carriers on a route was specified as an influence on the entry decision by carrier dummy variables. It may seem that the sign of the coefficients of these dummy variables should be negative—an additional carrier on a route reduces the likelihood of entry—but an appropriate interpretation is more complicated. The presence of a particular carrier was also taken into account in the fare variable. In addition, because carriers are not identical and thus may focus on different market niches (for example, a full-service network carrier catering to business travelers may attract entry on a route by a low-cost carrier catering to pleasure travelers) a positive sign is possible. The influence of a carrier's network on its entry decision was captured by a dummy variable that indicated whether the carrier has a hub at the origin or destination airport (*MYHUB*). The influence of its competitors' networks on its entry decision was captured by a dummy variable that indicated whether any of its competitors has a hub at the origin or destination airport (*OTHHUB*). *MYHUB* and *OTHHUB* should have positive and negative effects, respectively, on the likelihood of entry. The specification also accounted for the influence of fares on entry, as defined by the average fare in the market divided by a prediction from the carrier's fare regression of what the (nonincumbent) carrier would charge in that market (*RELFARE*). A carrier's expectation of being able to charge a higher fare, which lowers *RELFARE*, should increase the likelihood of its entry. *TPAX*, the total number of passengers on the route (including connecting passengers), accounts for the effect of actual traffic volume on entry, while the product of the origin and destination metropolitan area populations (*POP*) and the product of their real per capita incomes (*INC*) account for the effect of potential demand on entry. The higher that *TPAX*, *POP*, and *INC* are, the greater the likelihood of entry. Finally, we included the number of slot-constrained airports on the route (*SLOTS*) and one-way route distance (*DIST*). The presence of *SLOTS* on a route should decrease the likelihood of entry; the impact of *DIST* is likely to vary by carrier.

Estimation results for the entry models are shown in table 6-2. As in the fare regressions, the effects of the carrier presence dummy variables vary greatly. (Because the presence of carriers also influences entry through *RELFARE*, our interpretation of individual coefficients pro-

Table 6-2. Estimated Determinants of an Airline's Decision to Provide Direct Service on a Given Route[a]

Independent variable	Carrier									
	American	Alaska	Continental	Delta	America West	Northwest	TWA	United	USAir	Southwest
Constant	-1.905 (0.215)	-2.718 (0.483)	-2.426 (0.237)	-1.858 (0.231)	-1.359 (0.255)	-3.323 (0.216)	-2.582 (0.309)	-3.215 (0.240)	-2.437 (0.154)	-0.305 (0.288)
SLOTS	0.214 (0.081)	...	-0.003 (0.100)	0.100 (0.106)	-0.089 (0.119)	-0.040 (0.084)	0.463 (0.110)	0.255 (0.084)	-0.200 (0.074)	...
DIST	0.184 (0.040)	-0.653 (0.183)	0.191 (0.040)	-0.096 (0.046)	-0.127 (0.056)	0.141 (0.039)	-0.236 (0.074)	0.044 (0.043)	-0.172 (0.038)	-0.298 (0.077)
TPAX	0.184 (0.056)	0.022 (0.118)	0.146 (0.060)	0.196 (0.059)	0.039 (0.079)	0.034 (0.065)	-0.010 (0.076)	0.110 (0.090)	0.043 (0.049)	-0.201 (0.138)
RELFARE	-0.201 (0.110)	-0.468 (0.239)	-0.260 (0.125)	-0.228 (0.139)	-0.422 (0.119)	-0.056 (0.126)	-0.033 (0.128)	0.302 (0.138)	-0.179 (0.086)	-0.567 (0.090)
INC	-0.920 (0.407)	0.866 (0.920)	-0.444 (0.449)	-0.982 (0.489)	-1.613 (0.558)	2.089 (0.396)	0.320 (0.579)	0.352 (0.402)	2.094 (0.293)	-2.543 (0.651)
POP	-1.269 (1.571)	2.048 (4.119)	5.191 (1.084)	-1.142 (1.402)	3.425 (1.315)	3.285 (1.014)	1.308 (1.284)	-3.420 (1.357)	-0.051 (1.228)	5.877 (1.455)
American (presence dummy)	...	-0.161 (0.215)	-0.024 (0.106)	0.087 (0.099)	0.311 (0.105)	-0.115 (0.105)	0.018 (0.123)	0.016 (0.096)	-0.293 (0.083)	-0.329 (0.167)
Alaska (presence dummy)	0.067 (0.224)	...	0.150 (0.239)	0.279 (0.197)	0.059 (0.234)	0.159 (0.181)	-0.283 (0.370)	0.945 (0.136)	0.139 (0.124)	...
Continental (presence dummy)	0.160 (0.104)	...	...	-0.255 (0.138)	-0.014 (0.130)	-0.106 (0.103)	-0.142 (0.136)	0.431 (0.136)	-0.315 (0.124)	-0.237 (0.237)
Delta (presence dummy)	0.039 (0.082)	0.122 (0.205)	0.445 (0.084)	...	-0.048 (0.110)	0.068 (0.090)	0.269 (0.122)	-0.052 (0.093)	0.021 (0.072)	-0.204 (0.142)

	(1)	(2)	(3)	(4)	(5)	(6)	(7)	(8)	(9)	(10)
America West (presence dummy)	0.062 (0.127)	−0.318 (0.352)	−0.159 (0.178)	−0.048 (0.157)	⋯	−0.182 (0.190)	−0.173 (0.221)	−0.435 (0.241)	0.166 (0.098)	0.637 (0.131)
Northwest (presence dummy)	−0.004 (0.117)	⋯	0.161 (0.109)	−0.075 (0.117)	0.004 (0.134)	⋯	−0.024 (0.158)	0.155 (0.109)	−0.493 (0.105)	0.303 (0.141)
TWA (presence dummy)	0.014 (0.146)	−0.269 (0.395)	0.114 (0.126)	−0.193 (0.170)	0.219 (0.140)	0.021 (0.128)	⋯	−0.189 (0.156)	−0.230 (0.114)	0.557 (0.138)
United (presence dummy)	−0.223 (0.091)	0.346 (0.172)	0.115 (0.093)	−0.127 (0.111)	0.087 (0.116)	0.048 (0.096)	−0.003 (0.133)	⋯	−0.131 (0.082)	0.052 (0.171)
USAir (presence dummy)	−0.030 (0.092)	0.218 (0.170)	0.015 (0.092)	−0.291 (0.110)	−0.027 (0.119)	−0.307 (0.110)	−0.687 (0.183)	−0.300 (0.106)	⋯	0.187 (0.119)
Southwest (presence dummy)	−0.693 (0.180)	0.260 (0.312)	−0.038 (0.146)	−0.625 (0.199)	0.040 (0.126)	−1.005 (0.430)	−0.165 (0.173)	−1.344 (0.370)	−0.460 (0.115)	⋯
MYHUB	1.493 (0.086)	1.463 (0.254)	1.572 (0.083)	0.887 (0.082)	1.013 (0.131)	1.757 (0.107)	1.205 (0.120)	1.236 (0.075)	0.879 (0.088)	−0.025 (0.167)
OTHHUB	−0.258 (0.079)	−0.069 (0.175)	−0.279 (0.079)	−0.196 (0.082)	−0.358 (0.098)	−0.349 (0.079)	−0.453 (0.122)	−0.113 (0.088)	−0.183 (0.060)	−0.021 (0.106)
Summary statistic										
Number of observations	15,853	18,453	16,417	15,548	17,766	17,015	17,795	15,824	15,687	17,020
Log likelihood at zero	−1,214	−163	−1,053	−863	−612	−993	−512	−1,055	−1,503	−540
Log likelihood at convergence	−962	−138	−794	−737	−547	−776	−412	−813	−1,352	−462

Source: Authors' calculations; see text.

a. Standard errors in parentheses. Some variables were scaled so the coefficients would be of a similar order of magnitude. *POP* was divided by 10 to the fifteenth power, *INC* by 1 billion, *TPAX* by 10,000, and *DIST* by 1,000.

ceeds with the aforementioned caution.) Reading across the table, the presence of Southwest is a significant deterrent to many carriers from entering a market. USAir also discourages entry, possibly because of its aggressive response to new competition at Philadelphia and at airports in California. In contrast, Delta, Alaska, and America West do not discourage any carriers from entry; that is, their presence does not have any statistically significant effect on entry. In the case of Alaska and America West, this may be because they often do not lower their fares in response to the presence of other carriers (see table 6-1). The statistically significant effects of the other carriers are idiosyncratic: each discourages at least one carrier from entry but also encourages one. Although USAir generally discourages entry, it is also often discouraged by other carriers from entering markets. To a lesser extent this applies to Southwest, but Southwest also tends to enter markets because of the presence of certain carriers, especially America West and TWA. In accordance with their networks and operating characteristics, the remaining carriers are typically discouraged from entry by only a few carriers—Southwest usually being one of them—and occasionally encouraged to enter a market because of the presence of a particular carrier.

In general, carriers are attracted to markets where they have established a hub at the origin or destination and as their expected fare increases relative to the average fare. They are discouraged from entering markets where at least one of their competitors has established a hub at the origin or destination. As pointed out in chapter 4, although fares tend to be higher at hubs, the nondominant carrier is not typically able to receive a hub premium. The remaining influences on entry tend to vary in sign and statistical significance in accordance with a carrier's current network development and operating strategy. Thus, for example, Southwest is discouraged from entering markets with relatively high passenger volumes. This is consistent with its strategy of avoiding long-haul, high-density routes. American, United, and TWA are attracted to markets with a slot-controlled airport, even controlling for the fact that these carriers have hubs at these types of airports (American and United at O'Hare, TWA at Kennedy).

Exit from Routes

To complete our framework, we estimated a probit model of exit behavior using the same specifications as the entry model with the exception of *RELFARE*, which we defined as the average fare in the market divided by the actual fare the carrier charges in that market.[5] Of course, the expected sign of some of the variables was now reversed. The estimates in table 6-3 parallel many of those produced by the entry model. Southwest, USAir, and Northwest encourage many carriers to exit markets. Other carriers have idiosyncratic effects on a few carriers' exit behavior. Carriers are generally discouraged from exiting markets where they have established a hub at the origin or destination and as their fare increases relative to the average fare, but they are encouraged to exit markets where at least one of their competitors has established a hub at the origin or destination, although the magnitude and statistical significance of this effect is much smaller than in the entry model. In contrast to the entry model, high passenger volumes discourage carriers from exiting markets, but holding all else constant, carriers are more likely to exit long-haul markets, possibly because changes in the relation between fares and distance have made these markets less profitable than they once were, while short-haul markets have become more profitable.

Exit from the Industry

The fare, entry, and exit models were used to estimate the impact on fares of a carrier's exit from the industry. Assume, for instance, that America West failed to emerge from bankruptcy and underwent liquidation. The impact of America West's exit on other carriers' fares would initially be captured by the change in its carrier presence dummy in their fare equations. But this obviously would not be the end of the process because other carriers would enter and exit America West's markets in accordance with the impact of the change in America West's presence dummy and their relative fares (*RELFARE*). The entry and exit decisions of all carriers in response to America West's liquidation would in turn affect each carrier's fare as predicted by its fare equation. Carriers' entry and exit probabilities would again change in response to the change in *RELFARE* and the presence dummies. This process can be simulated

---

5. It could be argued that the actual fare is endogenous; its error term might be correlated with the error term in the exit equation because, for example, of omitted route characteristics that influence both variables. Thus we also defined *RELFARE* as we did in the entry equation: the average fare in the market divided by the predicted fare from the carrier's fare regression. As we discuss later, the effect of using this specification of *RELFARE* on the simulation results was negligible.

Table 6-3. Estimated Determinants of an Airline's Decision to Exit a Given Route[a]

Independent variable	Carrier									
	American	Alaska	Continental	Delta	America West	Northwest	TWA	United	USAir	Southwest
Constant	-2.364	-5.267	-1.972	-0.712	-1.816	-2.760	-0.682	-2.701	-3.591	-3.892
	(0.519)	(1.885)	(0.423)	(0.667)	(0.695)	(0.573)	(0.629)	(0.569)	(0.491)	(0.712)
SLOTS	0.348	···	-0.145	-0.068	0.210	0.194	0.387	0.185	-0.430	···
	(0.108)		(0.148)	(0.171)	(0.276)	(0.156)	(0.159)	(0.102)	(0.130)	
DIST	0.362	1.466	0.227	0.394	0.189	0.212	0.100	0.231	0.436	1.281
	(0.072)	(0.499)	(0.065)	(0.073)	(0.119)	(0.080)	(0.090)	(0.052)	(0.067)	(0.235)
TPAX	-0.238	-0.746	-0.512	-1.006	-0.776	-0.806	-0.311	-1.182	-0.670	-2.793
	(0.102)	(0.527)	(0.128)	(0.214)	(0.279)	(0.188)	(0.169)	(0.191)	(0.148)	(0.735)
RELFARE	1.998	2.664	1.224	0.588	0.770	2.961	0.679	1.503	1.976	0.765
	(0.402)	(1.269)	(0.296)	(0.568)	(0.441)	(0.418)	(0.295)	(0.512)	(0.436)	(0.448)
INC	-1.329	-0.316	0.642	-2.769	-1.264	-1.823	-2.320	0.397	0.224	2.145
	(0.604)	(2.190)	(0.571)	(0.704)	(1.234)	(0.761)	(0.936)	(0.529)	(0.515)	(1.637)
POP	-8.407	6.651	-1.823	3.343	4.028	-1.975	5.304	2.104	-0.640	-5.975
	(2.403)	(10.905)	(1.418)	(2.145)	(2.870)	(1.444)	(1.880)	(1.690)	(2.152)	(4.272)
American (presence dummy)	···	0.142	0.016	0.340	-0.022	0.075	0.319	-0.186	0.001	-0.151
		(0.377)	(0.157)	(0.116)	(0.234)	(0.202)	(0.194)	(0.120)	(0.148)	(0.454)
Alaska (presence dummy)	0.053	···	-0.479	0.190	0.781	-0.283	1.291	0.184	0.263	···
	(0.250)		(0.335)	(0.288)	(0.433)	(0.293)	(0.663)	(0.175)	(0.230)	
Continental (presence dummy)	-0.373	···	···	-0.040	0.236	0.244	0.372	0.270	0.010	-0.245
	(0.174)			(0.182)	(0.271)	(0.206)	(0.218)	(0.112)	(0.127)	(0.389)
Delta (presence dummy)	-0.032	-0.337	-0.108	···	0.182	0.235	-0.601	0.123	0.131	1.451
	(0.111)	(0.428)	(0.135)		(0.220)	(0.151)	(0.221)	(0.128)	(0.119)	(0.522)

America West (presence dummy)	0.086 (0.173)	−0.608 (0.631)	0.019 (0.244)	0.103 (0.227)	...	−0.104 (0.463)	−0.360 (0.320)	−0.585 (0.459)	0.264 (0.164)	0.396 (0.285)
Northwest (presence dummy)	0.234 (0.160)	...	−0.063 (0.165)	0.569 (0.137)	1.238 (0.319)	...	−0.032 (0.265)	0.435 (0.132)	0.406 (0.185)	1.506 (0.353)
TWA (presence dummy)	−0.535 (0.215)	3.258 (1.201)	0.027 (0.190)	0.349 (0.251)	0.355 (0.354)	0.164 (0.254)	...	...	0.570 (0.243)	0.279 (0.294)
United (presence dummy)	0.160 (0.111)	0.023 (0.299)	−0.177 (0.109)	−0.036 (0.156)	0.489 (0.259)	−0.351 (0.181)	−0.034 (0.208)	...	−0.003 (0.146)	−0.845 (0.740)
USAir (presence dummy)	0.058 (0.145)	0.904 (0.362)	0.415 (0.118)	0.424 (0.147)	−0.015 (0.261)	0.133 (0.186)	0.031 (0.224)	0.337 (0.150)	...	0.653 (0.462)
Southwest (presence dummy)	0.576 (0.341)	2.988 (1.219)	−0.408 (0.223)	0.993 (0.331)	0.554 (0.204)	...	−0.274 (0.258)	0.983 (0.316)	1.068 (0.219)	...
MYHUB	−1.119 (0.118)	−0.804 (0.348)	−1.372 (0.141)	−1.009 (0.121)	−1.219 (0.224)	−1.117 (0.124)	−0.850 (0.183)	−0.754 (0.113)	−0.670 (0.094)	−1.016 (0.262)
OTHHUB	−0.051 (0.118)	0.353 (0.350)	0.256 (0.100)	0.227 (0.108)	0.192 (0.184)	−0.205 (0.109)	0.102 (0.160)	0.114 (0.113)	0.070 (0.088)	0.206 (0.263)
Summary statistic										
Number of observations	3,147	547	2,583	3,452	1,234	1,985	1,205	3,176	3,313	1,980
Log likelihood at zero	−739	−95	−752	−617	−300	−568	−317	−722	−822	−214
Log likelihood at convergence	−585	−73	−613	−513	−223	−424	−270	−625	−715	−130

Source: Authors' calculations; see text.

a. Standard errors in parentheses. Some variables were scaled so the coefficients would be of a similar order of magnitude. *POP* was divided by 10 to the fifteenth power. *INC* by 1 billion, *TPAX* by 10,000, and *DIST* by 1,000.

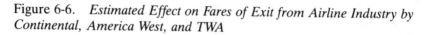

Figure 6-6. *Estimated Effect on Fares of Exit from Airline Industry by Continental, America West, and TWA*

Percent change

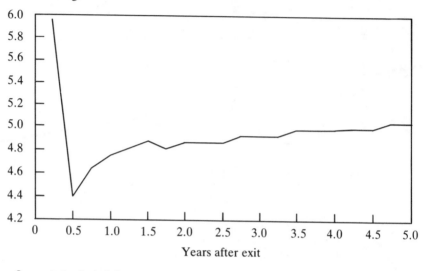

Years after exit

Source: Authors' calculations; see text.

for any length of time and can be used to analyze the impact on fares of any combination of carriers leaving the industry.

In our simulations we analyzed several situations in which individual carriers and combinations of carriers leave the industry. We ran the simulation process for twenty quarters, used the estimated coefficients from our base case, and used all estimated coefficients regardless of statistical significance. We assumed that no carriers other than the ten in our sample were able to enter and exit markets in response to a change in industry structure. By ignoring the competitive effects of new (low-cost) entrants such as Reno Air and any yet-to-be-formed entrants, we were overestimating the increase in fares when one or more carriers leaves the industry. We were also overestimating fare increases to the extent that we did not capture any major transformations in cost structure that any surviving carrier undergoes (for example, a high-cost carrier changes its operations and salary structure and becomes a low-cost carrier).

Figure 6-6 shows the time path of fare changes for a situation in which three carriers that have recently emerged from bankruptcy exit the industry. In this case and in the others we present, the fare changes are relative to what our simulations indicated would occur if no carriers exited the industry. In the first quarter, fares rise sharply because carriers have exited but other carriers have not had an opportunity to enter their markets. In the second quarter, carriers enter these markets, pushing fares down, but not as low as before the exit of the other carriers. During the next five quarters some carriers that entered the markets of the liquidated carriers reevaluate their decision and exit some of them, causing fares to rise.[6] At this point fares begin a slow upward drift.

The simulation results for all the situations, presented in table 6-4, show changes in fares, number of carriers, and market shares after twenty quarters. (As shown in appendix table 6A-2, the main conclusions are not particularly sensitive to the assumptions noted earlier.) Consumer welfare would not be seriously jeopardized by the departure of any carrier except Southwest, whose presence in a market, as shown in the fare equation, causes all its competitors to lower fares significantly. Therefore, as shown in the entry and exit equations, carriers do not like to compete with Southwest. Obviously, the rest of the industry would relish the opportunity to raise fares by 8.5 percent in the wake of Southwest's demise, at a cost to travelers of as much as $4 billion annually. That Southwest's departure would have such a large effect even though it would involve one of the smallest percentage reductions in the number of carriers per route shows that the identity of carriers in a market can be as important as their number. The exit of United or Delta would cause larger percentage reductions in the number of carriers per route than the exit of Southwest, but would cause industry fares to fall. The explanation, of course, is that United and Delta would be replaced by lower-cost carriers (as indicated by the changes in market shares) that would no longer be concerned with competing against an incumbent carrier with large capacity.

From the perspective of travelers' welfare, United's or Delta's departure could still be harmful if service frequency decreased. The small change in fares that would be caused by the departure of any of the other carriers appears to be consistent with the actual effect that liquidations have had on industry fare levels. Although many factors other than the exit of liquidated carriers cause fares to change, data from the Air Trans-

---

6. Although such behavior is reasonable, the overshoot that occurs in quarter two may simply reflect a quirk in the model. Because time is discrete, all airlines effectively make decisions simultaneously. Thus they cannot react to other airlines' intentions (via announcements, for example) but only to other carriers' actual entry and exit behavior.

Table 6-4. *Estimated Change in Fares, Airlines per Route, and Market Shares When One or More Airlines Exits the Industry, by Airline, Twenty Quarters after Exit*
Percent

Carriers exiting industry	Change in fares	Change in carriers per route	Change in carrier market shares									
			American	Alaska	Continental	Delta	America West	Northwest	TWA	United	USAir	Southwest
Continental	0.2	−9.2	8.7	5.9	−100.0	11.8	13.8	17.2	10.9	11.7	20.9	7.5
America West	3.1	−6.9	6.5	11.8	5.5	6.6	−100.0	5.4	3.6	4.5	10.9	15.0
TWA	1.4	−4.0	0.0	5.9	2.7	9.2	3.1	5.4	−100.0	10.6	8.2	3.8
Continental, America West, TWA	5.1	−20.7	17.4	23.5	−100.0	30.9	−100.0	30.1	−100.0	28.5	45.5	31.2
Alaska	−0.3	−1.7	0.7	−100.0	0.9	1.3	6.2	2.2	3.6	0.6	4.5	1.3
Southwest	8.5	−3.4	5.1	17.6	0.9	9.2	15.4	6.5	5.5	6.1	24.5	−100.0
Northwest	0.1	−4.6	9.4	5.9	5.5	9.9	16.9	−100.0	7.3	9.5	20.9	6.3
USAir	0.7	−6.9	9.4	11.8	9.1	17.1	13.8	16.1	25.5	8.9	−100.0	6.3
American	1.0	−10.3	−100.0	11.8	13.6	24.3	4.6	14.0	12.7	14.5	25.5	10.0
Delta	−1.4	−14.4	19.6	5.9	4.5	−100.0	24.6	18.3	1.8	20.1	31.8	18.8
United	−2.2	−6.3	32.6	5.9	16.4	13.8	35.4	6.5	49.1	−100.0	31.8	6.3
Alaska, Continental, America West, Northwest, TWA, USAir, Southwest	24.2	−49.4	84.8	−100.0	−100.0	164.5	−100.0	−100.0	−100.0	91.6	−100.0	−100.0
Alaska, Continental, America West, TWA, USAir	8.6	−40.8	67.4	−100.0	−100.0	109.9	−100.0	−100.0	−100.0	69.3	−100.0	83.8
Alaska, Continental, America West, TWA, USAir, Southwest	21.7	−40.8	51.4	−100.0	−100.0	111.8	−100.0	−100.0	−100.0	63.1	−100.0	−100.0

Source: Authors' calculations; see text.

port Association show, for example, that three months after Pan American's liquidation fares rose by 0.5 percent compared with fares in the same month one year earlier. Three months after Eastern's liquidation fares fell by 4.5 percent compared with fares in the same month one year earlier.[7]

Table 6-4 also shows the effects of simulations in which several carriers leave the industry. If the carriers that recently emerged from bankruptcy (Continental, TWA, and America West) were liquidated, fares would increase by about 5.1 percent (as in figure 6-6). If, however, a disaster would occur and American, United, and Delta were the only carriers remaining in the industry, fares would rise 24.2 percent. But even in this case fares would only return to where they would likely have been under regulation (see chapter 2), and, of course, even the industry's most constant doomsayers would not include Southwest among the airlines that fail. If Southwest joined American, United, and Delta as survivors, the fare increase is 8.6 percent, which still preserves most of the fare decrease due to deregulation. If Northwest Airlines rather than Southwest remained in the industry with the big three, fares would rise by 21.7 percent, again demonstrating Southwest's unparalleled ability to discipline competitors.[8]

A final set of simulations involves carrier consolidations (table 6-5). The acquired carrier (Northwest, for example) takes on the characteristics of the acquiring carrier (American, for example). Thus American's presence dummy in the fare equations takes on a value of 1 for those routes where Northwest is present (Northwest's presence dummy takes on a value of zero), and Northwest's behavior is reflected in American's fare, entry, and exit equations. Finally, Northwest's hubs become American's hubs. We also considered some consolidations motivated by potential international network expansion. That is, American, United, or Delta acquires Northwest with the expectation of developing Asian routes, and American, United, or USAir acquires TWA with the expectation of developing European routes.

Because carrier networks and interactions could change more dramatically in response to a merger than we were able show, our findings

7. Air Transport Association, *Monthly Discount Report* (various issues).

8. The findings barely changed when we ran the simulations using the exit model estimated with the fitted *RELFARE* variable. The largest change in the effect on fares was 1.1 percentage points after twenty-one quarters. The average effect was 0.4 percentage points.

Table 6-5. *Estimated Change in Fares, Airlines per Route, and Market Shares Caused by Selected Mergers, One and Twenty-One Quarters after Merger*

Percent unless otherwise specified

Merger	Elapsed quarters	Change in fares	Change in carriers per route	Change in carrier market shares									
				American	Alaska	Continental	Delta	America West	Northwest	TWA	United	USAir	Southwest
American and Northwest	1	1.5	-1.6	58.1	0	1.7	0.7	0	-100.0	2.0	1.7	0	1.1
	21	-1.9	10.9	15.2	17.6	13.6	4.6	26.2	-100.0	9.1	10.6	5.5	1.3
American and TWA	1	1.2	-1.6	26.5	0	0.9	2.1	0	1.0	-100.0	2.3	0	0
	21	-2.9	20.7	18.1	23.5	27.3	-17.1	29.2	29.0	-100.0	-11.7	0.9	-3.8
Delta and Northwest	1	1.9	-1.6	13.1	6.3	3.6	55.6	-4.6	-100.0	-12.3	1.1	-10.7	6.0
	21	-1.9	12.1	1.3	17.6	8.7	16.1	30.6	-100.0	24.5	10.9	17.2	-9.1
United and Northwest	1	0.7	-2.2	16.1	6.3	4.5	-4.0	-4.6	-100.0	-12.3	51.1	-10.7	6.0
	21	-1.7	11.5	1.3	23.5	8.7	11.2	30.6	-100.0	20.4	15.4	17.2	-8.0
United and TWA	1	1.3	-1.6	16.8	6.3	3.6	-3.3	-4.6	4.3	-100.0	23.6	-11.6	6.0
	21	-2.9	20.7	3.9	29.4	21.7	-11.9	35.5	23.7	-100.0	-8.6	11.1	-12.5
USAir and TWA	1	0.4	-1.1	0	0	0	2.1	0	0	-100.0	0	47.5	0
	21	-3.1	20.7	17.4	23.5	27.3	-18.4	29.2	29.0	-100.0	-12.3	3.6	-3.8

Source: Authors' calculations; see text.

are only suggestive. Nonetheless, the effects of the consolidations follow a similar pattern. In the first quarter, without any entry and exit by other carriers, the consolidated carrier raises the industry fare level, but following twenty quarters of entry, exit, and fare changes by all carriers, fares fall to 2 or 3 percent below the premerger level.[9] The explanation for this finding is now familiar: the void created by an initial reduction in capacity would eventually be filled by lower-cost carriers who would put downward pressure on fares.[10] This obviously suggests that merger evaluations by the federal government should consider potential entrants into markets affected by a merger as well as the networks of the prospective partners.

The International Dimension

Although the simulations we performed covered only U.S. airlines, the U.S. industry's evolution will undoubtedly be influenced by changes in international airline competition. And although Canada, Australia, New Zealand, and Japan have also (at least partially) deregulated airline competition within their borders, international airline competition is still governed by negotiations between countries. At the 1944 Chicago convention, the United States sought to establish multilateral agreements whereby market forces would primarily determine fares and capacities on international routes, an interesting proposition given that domestic competition was heavily regulated by the Civil Aeronautics Board.[11] But the effort failed, and ever since, bilateral agreements have provided the framework under which fares and service frequency between country pairs are determined.

9. The initial rise in fares from a merger is consistent with retrospective studies of actual mergers, but these studies have not explicitly modeled the long-run entry, exit, and fare changes following a merger; see, for example, Gregory J. Werden, Andrew S. Joskow, and Richard L. Johnson, "The Effects of Mergers on Price and Output: Two Case Studies from the Airline Industry," *Managerial and Decision Economics*, vol. 12 (October 1991), pp. 341–52; and Steven A. Morrison and Clifford Winston, "Enhancing the Performance of the Deregulated Air Transportation System," *Brookings Papers on Economic Activity: Microeconomics* (1989), pp. 61–112.

10. The findings were nearly identical when we ran the simulations using the exit model estimated with the fitted *RELFARE* variable. The largest change in the effect on fares was 0.2 percentage point after twenty-one quarters. The average effect was 0.1 percentage point.

11. For a complete discussion of the evolution of international airline policy see David H. Good, Lars-Hendrik Roller, and Robin C. Sickles, "U.S. Airline Deregulation: Implications for European Transport," *Economic Journal*, vol. 103 (July 1993), pp. 1028–41.

The Carter administration promoted an open skies policy, liberal bilateral agreements that freed market forces to be the most important determinants of fares and capacity. The United States has negotiated these agreements with more than twenty countries, but restrictive agreements between the United States and many other countries, particularly in Europe, still exist. Nevertheless, there is cause for optimism. In Europe, for example, carriers from the European Union countries can, subject to gate and slot availability, offer service to any member country, usually at any fare they desire. In 1997 these carriers will be able to compete on member countries' domestic routes as well. The United States continues to press for open skies one country at a time, concluding a successful agreement with the Netherlands in 1992 and agreeing with Canada in late 1994 to eliminate route restrictions between the two countries. Agreements with one or two European countries may well expand the United States-European market considerably if flying across Europe is open sky.

Negotiations appear to stall when countries are concerned that their carriers will not be able to compete without large subsidies against more efficient American carriers. It is estimated, for example, that American carriers have a 28 percent labor productivity advantage over European carriers.[12] Other stumbling blocks arise when American carriers argue that the large U.S. market enables foreign carriers to gain access to more potential passengers than U.S. carriers would in foreign markets. U.S. carriers also argue that they would be at a disadvantage if they had to compete against heavily subsidized foreign carriers.

While politics and negotiations are running their course, the major global carriers are positioning themselves for unregulated international competition. The big three U.S. carriers have been trying to expand and develop their European and Asian presence: Delta has purchased most of Pan American's European routes, United has purchased Pan American's Asian routes and routes to London, and American has purchased TWA's routes to London. U.S. carriers are also entering into marketing alliances with non-U.S. carriers and selling or buying partial ownership. Northwest has sold part of its company to KLM and USAir part of its to British Air, while American has bought part of Canadian Airlines Inter-

12. This estimate is from a McKinsey study cited in "Survey: Airlines," *Economist*, June 12, 1993, p. 18.

national. Some foreign carriers have acquired interests in other foreign carriers (Air France acquired 37.5 percent of Sabena) or gone private (Air Canada, British Air, Japan Air, QANTAS) to improve their competitiveness.

Although we can only speculate, airline competition brought about by global deregulation will probably parallel domestic deregulation's effects and benefit American consumers and carriers (see table 2-3 in chapter 2). To estimate how much travelers would benefit from a deregulated international air transport regime, we used the Department of Transportation's Data Bank 1A ticket sample to calculate what round-trip fares for international markets (including Canada and Mexico) involving a U.S. city would be if they equaled U.S. domestic average fares for markets of the same distances. After accounting for different taxation of domestic and international trips, domestic fares turned out to be 28 percent lower, on average, than international fares, which implies that passengers flying on U.S. airlines would gain $4.2 billion in 1993 dollars from international deregulation.[13] Fares on domestic pleasure routes could also decrease to the extent that they align with sharply discounted fares on international pleasure routes; this decrease would discourage travelers from substituting a foreign vacation for a domestic one. Finally, fares on many domestic routes should fall to the extent that foreign carriers are able to enter U.S. routes to feed their international traffic (cabotage). Expanded competition from abroad should partially offset any reduction in competition among domestic airlines, which makes the disaster situation in which there would be only three major competitors in the domestic market very unlikely.

Because of their productivity advantages and experience with competing in a deregulated environment, most U.S. carriers would benefit from being able to compete for millions of additional travelers worldwide despite the prospect of more competition on their domestic routes. As discussed later, U.S. carriers would make significant adjustments to their route structures and operations in pursuit of these benefits.

13. The aggregate savings to passengers flying on U.S. airlines would be 27.6 percent of U.S. airlines' 1993 international passenger revenue of $15.2 billion. Savings to passengers flying on other countries' carriers as well as the benefits to those travelers who are induced to travel by the lower fares would be additional. But our procedure may be somewhat optimistic because the longest-haul domestic markets (trips to mainland Hawaii) that served as the basis for some of our comparisons have a large percentage of low-fare vacation travelers.

Figure 6-7.   *Indexes of Real Revenues and Costs per Revenue-Ton Mile,
1970–93*

Index (1977 = 100)

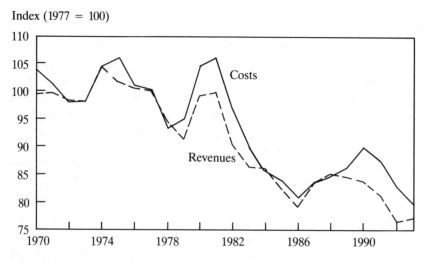

Source: Nominal airline costs and revenues are from Air Transport Association, *Air Transport: The
Annual Report of the U.S. Scheduled Airline Industry* (Washington, various years). Data were converted
to real terms using the consumer price index.

Toward Long-Run Equilibrium

The airline industry's evolution continues to be governed by a long-term decline in real fares and costs spurred by technological and operational advances and greater competition (figure 6-7). Since 1989, however, carriers have had difficulty aligning fares with costs, raising concern about the long-run financial viability of the industry.

In the competitive deregulated environment, industry equilibrium is achieved when carriers' fares generate a normal rate of return. But because carriers are unlikely to sustain fare increases, given the future we envision for the industry, equilibrium can be reached only if they can lower their costs. (Indeed, our entry, exit, and pricing model predicts airfares will fall by another 3 percent in the next five years, assuming there are no changes in current industry structure.)[14]

Downward pressure on fares could be even greater if air travel comes to be dominated by the more price-sensitive pleasure travelers. Histori-

14. The explanation for this finding appears to be general competitive pressures. That is, an inspection of the detailed results of the simulation did not reveal any specific explanation such as growth in the share of low-cost carriers at the expense of the other carriers.

cally, the pleasure and business shares of air travel have each been 50 percent. But in the past few years the share of business travel has decreased, possibly because faxes, teleconferencing, and other products of information technology have eliminated the need for many business trips.[15] It is, of course, premature to conclude that the recent changes portend any long-term trend. If such a trend were to develop, however, and carriers tried to raise fares for the remaining business travel, yet more substitution of information technology for air travel and more negotiated fares between corporations and airlines could result.

To attain long-run financial viability, carriers are trying to reduce costs. Indeed, it appears that every one of them is trying to become a so-called low-cost carrier. Southwest Airlines has served as the model by pioneering low-cost, short- to medium-haul operations with high labor productivity, few frills service, fast turnaround time at relatively uncongested airports to maximize aircraft utilization, and less reliance on hub-and-spoke operations.[16] But Southwest's operations cannot be the model for the whole industry. Its point-to-point strategy works best on dense short-haul routes. Long-haul and international routes are where larger aircraft and the hub-and-spoke system achieve their greatest effect. Still, carriers specializing in long-haul service can reduce costs by negotiating fewer work restrictions to increase flexibility in the use of labor and by subcontracting out certain airport operations. Finally, all carriers can potentially lower costs through such innovations as replacing airline tickets with so-called smart cards that automate some functions now performed by ticket agents.[17] Carriers are also trying to reduce travel agent commissions. Whether these reductions can be maintained in the face of possible losses in revenue from travel agents who attempt to divert passengers from the flights of particular carriers remains to be seen.

Carriers are likely to rely on two strategies for developing their networks: the Southwest model for shorter routes and the hub-and-spoke

15. According to Gallup polls for the Air Transport Association, in 1991 the pleasure and business travel share was 54–46, in 1992 it was 63–37, and in 1993 it was 52–48. See Gallup Organization, *Air Travel Survey* (Washington: Air Transport Association of America, various years).

16. Southwest does some hubbing, as the presence of connecting routes in figure 6-1 indicates. From Department of Transportation Data Bank 1A we calculated that in 1993 11 percent of passengers boarding Southwest flights were making connections. This compares with 29 percent for the industry as a whole.

17. See Frank Swoboda, "Technology's the Ticket," *Washington Post*, November 20, 1994.

for longer domestic and international routes. The global American carriers are likely to focus on international and long-haul domestic operations, while regional carriers, new entrants, and possibly downsized major carriers or low-cost subsidiaries of global carriers will compete on shorter domestic routes. United Airlines has recently introduced, and USAir is planning to introduce, a low-cost service for short-haul routes that emulates Southwest's operations.[18]

Given that labor is the largest category of costs (34.8 percent in 1993, according to the Air Transport Association) and that they are more controllable, airlines are also looking to labor to reduce costs and improve productivity. Since administrative deregulation in 1976, average hourly wages in the airline industry have risen more slowly than wages in manufacturing and the transportation-public utility sectors. From 1977 to 1990 average hourly wages rose 65 percent (from $7.74 to $12.74) in air transportation, 87 percent (from $6.94 to $12.95) in the transportation–public utility sector, and 91 percent (from $5.68 to $10.84) in manufacturing. As a share of total airline operating expenses, labor costs fell from 42 percent in 1978 to 33 percent in 1990, even with decreasing fuel prices.[19] But in the face of stronger union bargaining power and rising average wages because less senior, lower-paid workers are being laid off, airlines are going to be hard pressed to maintain this trend.[20] Carriers will therefore have to explore ways to increase productivity, not only to lower costs, but because service is an especially important aspect of international airline competition, one area in which U.S. carriers are judged inferior to foreign carriers, especially the Asian, West European, and Scandinavian airlines.

Some observers believe that labor productivity can be increased by giving workers greater participation in workplace decisions. Work rules, for example, can be changed to provide employees with financial incentives for suggestions that result in cost savings and allow them to perform several tasks as part of a team, the approach taken by Southwest Airlines. A more extreme idea is to allow workers to own and manage the airline, as in the case of United Airlines' employee buyout, but it is not clear

18. Continental introduced but then dropped its low-fare service called Continental Lite.

19. See Office of the Secretary of Transportation, *Labor Relations and Labor Costs in the Airline Industry: Contemporary Issues* (Department of Transportation, May 1992), pp. 29, 31.

20. For a full discussion of the factors behind rising union bargaining power see Office of the Secretary of Transportation, *Labor Relations and Labor Costs.*

that this action will lower labor costs and that the industry will pursue it. But it should be increasingly clear to labor that because the industry is so competitive under deregulation, wages can be increased only if productivity increases. Thus management and labor will have strong incentives to increase productivity.

Notwithstanding cost reductions from network restructuring and improved labor productivity, carriers must do a better job of minimizing the disruptions to their long-term growth caused by the business cycle. The obvious but not easy way to do this is to make better forecasts of the economy. Indeed, when we updated the forecasting model presented in chapter 5, we found that if the economy performs as predicted by the Livingston survey in 1994 and 1995, the forecast error will be small and predicted industry gross margins will be 3.4 percent for 1994 and 3.6 percent for 1995, levels approaching that of a healthy industry.[21]

Technological change will undoubtedly continue to influence the industry's evolution. It is difficult, however, to imagine the next innovation whose impact will rival the development of jet aircraft or high-bypass engines, especially because recent cuts in military research and development decrease the likelihood of commercial spin-offs.[22] As a matter of speculation, a breakthrough in supersonic transport technology that would allow these aircraft to meet environmental standards for flight over land and sea, in concert with innovations that reduce their cost and lengthen their range, could lead to even more network restructuring.[23] Hub-and-spoke operations would then be used for international travel, while more domestic travel would be able to be served point to point because more daily round-trips on long-haul routes would be possible.

21. These predictions are based on forecasts of GDP growth for 1994 and 1995 of 3.84 percent and 2.78 percent from the Livingston survey, an average of the forecasts of several forecasters, available from the Federal Reserve Bank of Philadelphia.

22. The military has been interested in commercial uses for some of its aircraft, particularly the tiltrotor, which has the seating capacity of a commuter plane and makes vertical takeoffs and landings like a helicopter. The alleged social benefit of this craft is that it can reduce congestion at major airports and commuting time from them by operating from vertiports, which do not require much "runway" capacity, in a city center or another part of the existing airport. However, the operating cost of this craft is significantly higher than that of a comparable commuter plane, its safety record is weak, and commercial carriers' interest in it has been minimal.

23. Recently a patent was granted for a design that could enable a supersonic jet to fly without creating much of a sonic boom and thus make flights over land. See Teresa Riordan, "Patents," *New York Times*, March 7, 1994.

Conclusion

Even under the most disastrous scenario for the deregulated industry's evolution, travelers will be no worse off than they would have been had regulation continued under its established rules. And there are reasons to believe that travelers' welfare will actually improve as the industry evolves.

Given the industry's recent financial performance, a more serious concern for policymakers is the carriers' welfare, which has been deteriorating since the beginning of the 1990s. Fortunately, improving airline profits need not come at the expense of travelers. In accordance with historical trends and the current costs of investment, the industry's long-run financial viability depends on carriers' lowering their costs, leading to even lower fares. Indeed, airlines are taking measures to lower costs by restructuring their networks and improving labor productivity. Furthermore, by reducing their exposure to the destabilizing influences of the business cycle through better forecasts and more prudent expansion decisions, and by exploiting the potential for growth in international markets, they will also be able to stabilize their revenues. Global deregulation could spur greater improvements in efficiency and generate some $4.2 billion annually in benefits to passengers from lower fares on U.S. airlines alone.

Appendix

This appendix sets out the full estimation results of each carrier's fare equation (table 6A-1) and sensitivity tests of the simulation results (table 6A-2). The base-case procedures and assumptions for the simulations were that the simulation process runs twenty quarters, a carrier has entered a market if it provides at least one flight a day (low limit is equal to 600 sampled passengers in a quarter), and all coefficients were used regardless of significance level (significance level is equal to 1.00).

Table 6A-1. Estimation Results of Fare Equations, by Airline[a]

Independent variable	Carrier									
	American	Alaska	Continental	Delta	America West	Northwest	TWA	United	USAir	Southwest
Constant	-0.898 (0.188)	3.09 (0.147)	1.024 (0.142)	0.938 (0.163)	2.502 (0.183)	2.966 (0.170)	-0.051 (0.280)	3.147 (0.120)	1.909 (0.143)	1.144 (0.110)
Slot dummy (Washington National Airport)	0.177 (0.031)	...	0.128 (0.027)	0.070 (0.017)	0.148 (0.030)	-0.042 (0.014)	0.028 (0.030)	0.072 (0.019)	0.063 (0.011)	...
Slot dummy (JFK Airport)	-0.189 (0.039)	...	...	-0.253 (0.033)	0.063 (0.032)	0.122 (0.049)	-0.265 (0.028)	0.193 (0.031)	...	...
Slot dummy (LaGuardia Airport)	-0.046 (0.030)	...	0.021 (0.022)	-0.064 (0.022)	...	-0.037 (0.022)	-0.042 (0.031)	0.040 (0.023)	0.006 (0.015)	...
Slot dummy (Chicago O'Hare Airport)	0.037 (0.020)	...	0.076 (0.035)	-0.084 (0.028)	-0.062 (0.042)	-0.187 (0.052)	-0.346 (0.051)	0.131 (0.013)	0.527 (0.027)	...
Log distance (one-way miles)	0.511 (0.010)	0.548 (0.022)	0.375 (0.008)	0.324 (0.008)	0.412 (0.009)	0.186 (0.010)	0.426 (0.016)	0.348 (0.008)	0.260 (0.006)	0.590 (0.008)
Log product of origin and destination population	0.091 (0.006)	-0.054 (0.004)	0.053 (0.004)	0.074 (0.005)	-0.015 (0.006)	0.034 (0.005)	0.079 (0.009)	-0.009 (0.004)	0.050 (0.004)	-0.014 (0.004)
American presence dummy	...	-0.037 (0.034)	-0.210 (0.021)	-0.209 (0.014)	-0.053 (0.021)	-0.108 (0.028)	-0.044 (0.030)	-0.008 (0.012)	-0.138 (0.019)	-0.068 (0.062)
Alaska presence dummy	0.054 (0.031)	...	-0.180 (0.056)	-0.164 (0.033)	0.191 (0.034)	-0.168 (0.032)	-0.606 (0.051)	0.094 (0.023)	-0.127 (0.037)	-0.063 (0.081)

Continental presence dummy	−0.192	−0.201	· · ·	−0.079	0.018	−0.030	−0.095	0.061	−0.008	0.123
	(0.021)	(0.058)		(0.018)	(0.029)	(0.021)	(0.034)	(0.009)	(0.014)	(0.030)
Delta presence dummy	−0.072	0.084	−0.022	· · ·	0.071	−0.109	−0.248	−0.037	−0.145	−0.034
	(0.014)	(0.030)	(0.017)		(0.020)	(0.016)	(0.027)	(0.012)	(0.014)	(0.029)
America West presence dummy	−0.227	−0.183	−0.188	−0.133	· · ·	−0.210	−0.169	−0.184	−0.381	−0.248
	(0.019)	(0.028)	(0.023)	(0.024)		(0.027)	(0.045)	(0.019)	(0.023)	(0.013)
Northwest presence dummy	−0.162	0.047	−0.076	−0.085	0.023	· · ·	−0.103	−0.092	0.052	−0.145
	(0.029)	(0.037)	(0.023)	(0.017)	(0.038)		(0.047)	(0.018)	(0.021)	(0.036)
TWA presence dummy	−0.170	0.160	−0.159	−0.156	0.021	−0.178	· · ·	−0.065	−0.033	−0.095
	(0.038)	(0.198)	(0.029)	(0.022)	(0.033)	(0.050)		(0.029)	(0.027)	(0.016)
United presence dummy	0.001	0.079	0.118	0.040	0.107	−0.014	−0.056	· · ·	−0.237	−0.178
	(0.019)	(0.026)	(0.010)	(0.017)	(0.029)	(0.019)	(0.026)		(0.018)	(0.026)
USAir presence dummy	−0.046	0.026	0.064	−0.231	−0.047	−0.115	−0.146	−0.122	· · ·	−0.117
	(0.019)	(0.031)	(0.017)	(0.014)	(0.019)	(0.023)	(0.041)	(0.018)		(0.023)
Southwest presence dummy	−0.350	−1.052	−0.315	−0.740	−0.404	−0.625	−0.495	−0.713	−0.628	· · ·
	(0.072)	(0.096)	(0.034)	(0.062)	(0.014)	(0.067)	(0.028)	(0.031)	(0.026)	
Summary statistic										
R^2	0.59	0.68	0.56	0.52	0.79	0.37	0.71	0.58	0.59	0.74
Number of observations	3,322	575	2,711	3,631	1,308	2,082	1,264	3,339	3,484	2,105

Source: Authors' calculations.
a. Heteroskedastic-consistent standard errors in parentheses. Dependent variable is log real fare.

Table 6A-2. *Sensitivity Tests of Simulation Results*

Carriers exiting industry	Low limit	Percentage change in fares after twenty quarters (significance level)				Percentage change in fares after forty quarters (significance level)			
		1.00	*0.10*	*0.05*	*0.01*	*1.00*	*0.10*	*0.05*	*0.01*
Continental	100	4.2	3.9	4.6	4.8	4.2	3.7	4.7	5.1
	300	1.0	1.1	1.2	1.1	0.9	1.3	1.5	1.4
	600	0.2	-0.3	-0.5	0.9	0.1	-0.6	-1.1	0.6
	900	-0.6	0.2	0.3	0.4	-0.9	0.2	0.3	0.5
Minimum and maximum		-0.6	4.8			-1.1	5.1		
America West	100	4.5	5.6	9.0	8.3	4.6	8.0	11.5	10.6
	300	4.0	4.9	5.5	5.8	4.3	5.4	5.9	6.2
	600	3.1	3.4	6.2	0.9	3.2	3.4	8.0	1.3
	900	2.1	2.4	2.6	2.7	2.2	2.5	3.1	2.9
Minimum and maximum		0.9	9.0			1.3	11.5		
TWA	100	3.7	4.6	5.7	3.7	4.2	6.2	7.0	4.4
	300	2.0	2.6	2.1	1.9	2.2	3.5	2.6	2.3
	600	1.4	1.2	1.1	0.9	1.5	1.5	1.2	0.9
	900	1.3	1.7	1.8	1.5	1.3	1.7	1.8	1.6
Minimum and maximum		0.9	5.7			0.9	7.0		
Continental, America West, TWA	100	13.2	16.6	20.4	17.4	13.9	18.2	24.2	20.6
	300	7.5	8.7	9.2	9.5	8.3	10.2	10.4	10.7
	600	5.1	4.6	7.3	2.6	5.3	4.8	8.0	2.8
	900	3.2	4.8	5.2	5.5	2.9	5.0	5.7	5.7
Minimum and maximum		2.6	20.4			2.8	24.2		
Alaska	100	-0.4	-0.4	-0.3	-0.4	-0.4	-0.4	-0.3	-0.5
	300	-0.2	-0.1	0.1	1.1	-0.2	0.2	0.5	2.0
	600	-0.3	-0.2	-0.2	0.3	-0.3	-0.2	-0.1	0.8
	900	-0.5	-0.6	-0.4	-0.1	-0.5	-0.5	-0.5	0.0
Minimum and maximum		-0.6	1.1			-0.8	2.0		
Southwest	100	8.4	10.4	14.5	13.7	9.3	13.2	20.4	19.1
	300	8.8	17.9	17.0	15.1	9.6	25.3	23.4	19.1
	600	8.5	17.0	21.7	22.2	8.9	22.0	30.3	31.4
	900	8.7	9.8	9.9	8.0	9.3	11.0	11.1	9.4
Minimum and maximum		8.0	22.2			8.9	31.4		
Northwest	100	3.9	3.4	4.0	3.9	3.8	2.9	3.9	3.5
	300	0.6	0.9	-0.1	-0.2	0.4	1.1	-0.5	-0.9
	600	0.1	0.0	0.3	-0.1	-0.2	-0.4	0.3	-0.4
	900	-0.5	-0.3	-0.2	-0.1	-0.8	-0.4	-0.2	-0.1
Minimum and maximum		-0.5	4.0			-0.9	3.9		

Table 6A-2. *(Continued)*

Carriers exiting industry	Low limit	Percentage change in fares after twenty quarters (significance level)				Percentage change in fares after forty quarters (significance level)			
		1.00	*0.10*	*0.05*	*0.01*	*1.00*	*0.10*	*0.05*	*0.01*
USAir	100	4.0	2.3	2.9	2.6	4.3	2.4	3.2	2.3
	300	1.9	1.2	1.2	1.8	1.8	0.9	1.0	1.8
	600	0.7	0.3	0.0	1.9	0.7	0.0	-0.4	1.5
	900	0.9	0.7	1.0	0.9	1.0	0.9	1.2	1.0
Minimum and maximum		0.0	4.0			-0.4	4.3		
American	100	8.3	7.8	8.2	8.8	8.8	8.2	9.2	10.1
	300	2.4	1.6	1.7	1.8	2.5	1.4	1.5	1.4
	600	1.0	-0.5	-1.0	2.0	1.0	-1.0	-2.1	1.7
	900	1.4	2.8	3.0	2.4	1.6	2.6	3.0	2.3
Minimum and maximum		-1.0	8.8			-2.1	10.1		
Delta	100	0.7	-0.4	1.7	2.3	0.0	-1.7	1.6	2.4
	300	-1.7	-3.7	-3.5	-3.0	-2.5	-4.1	-4.0	-3.9
	600	-1.4	-2.7	-1.0	2.3	-2.1	-3.5	-1.0	2.2
	900	-1.8	-1.1	-1.1	-1.2	-2.7	-1.3	-1.3	-1.1
Minimum and maximum		-3.7	2.3			-4.1	2.4		
United	100	-1.3	-0.5	1.0	-0.6	-1.2	-0.1	2.1	-0.4
	300	-2.1	-2.3	-2.2	-1.7	-2.5	-2.6	-2.8	2.3
	600	-2.2	-2.9	-3.8	-8.7	-2.1	-2.9	-4.1	-9.0
	900	-1.5	-6.6	-5.5	-4.8	-1.7	-7.1	-8.0	-4.6
Minimum and maximum		-8.7	1.0			-9.0	2.1		
Alaska, Continental, America West, Northwest, TWA, USAir, Southwest	100	31.8	35.7	42.6	39.8	33.2	39.5	50.9	47.3
	300	26.8	36.6	36.3	36.1	26.5	46.1	44.7	43.2
	600	24.2	33.9	41.1	36.7	25.3	39.8	53.8	47.0
	900	23.3	25.2	26.9	25.3	24.5	26.9	26.8	27.3
Minimum and maximum		23.3	42.6			24.5	53.8		
Alaska, Continental, America West, Northwest, TWA, USAir	100	20.5	22.3	27.2	24.0	21.1	23.6	31.1	26.6
	300	12.8	12.7	12.4	14.1	13.1	14.6	13.7	16.2
	600	8.6	6.0	9.0	6.2	9.0	6.3	11.0	8.5
	900	4.0	6.5	7.8	9.4	4.4	7.4	8.9	10.1
Minimum and maximum		4.0	27.2			4.4	31.1		
Alaska, Continental, America West, TWA, USAir, Southwest	100	26.6	32.3	38.7	35.7	30.0	35.9	46.7	42.9
	300	24.5	34.8	34.9	34.8	26.1	44.1	43.1	41.4
	600	21.7	30.5	38.4	34.5	22.4	36.2	50.7	45.4
	900	21.3	23.3	24.7	23.2	22.1	24.8	26.6	25.1
Minimum and maximum		21.3	38.7			22.1	50.7		

Source: Authors' calculations.

CHAPTER SEVEN

Policy Implications

As DEREGULATION has evolved, the U.S. airline industry has become more competitive, generally providing travelers with lower fares and more frequent service. Although industry leadership has changed hands from the established carriers to new entrants, back to the established carriers, and lately to low-cost carriers, it has become increasingly clear that airlines cannot count on exploiting opportunities to charge and maintain high fares to remain profitable. Indeed, the alleged anticompetitive effects of innovations such as computer reservation systems, hub-and-spoke operations, yield management, and frequent flier programs are minor or can be overcome. Often the innovations actually benefit most travelers.

The primary source of the industry's financial troubles is not structural factors that prevent it from earning a normal rate of return for a sustained period but its failure to adapt efficiently to the business cycle. To be sure, forecasting problems and consequent overcapacity may have occurred because as a formerly regulated industry airlines suddenly had a lot to learn: the management techniques used under regulation did not transfer very well to a deregulated environment. As the industry evolves toward its long-run equilibrium, it will make improvements in its capacity decisions and take appropriate measures to lower costs and stabilize revenues without raising real fares or compromising safety. In short, although the ride has hardly been smooth, the industry is moving in the right direction.

In the process of reaching this conclusion, we have illustrated the pitfalls of failing to take a long-run view of the industry. The conclusions from studies on a variety of topics, including the effect of airline competition on the spread of fares and the effect of hubs and multimarket contact on levels of fares, change when they are subjected to an analysis that covers a longer time.

In principle, public policy toward the airline industry could be constructive if it expedited industry evolution and, where appropriate, fine-tuned it. Experience shows, however, that although the industry has had close ties to the federal government since its inception, it is better for government to keep its hands off. We have uncovered no evidence that justifies reregulation, new regulations, or a more activist antitrust policy.

Nonetheless, public and official concern over the industry's large losses led to the creation in April 1993 of the National Commission to Ensure a Strong Competitive Airline Industry. That the commission did not call for major new regulations or reregulation can be seen as implicit support for the conclusions we have reached.[1] It is useful, however, to pursue briefly some issues raised in the report and some others worthy of attention.

Government Intervention

The national commission recommended some steps that the federal government could take to improve industry performance. It recommended, for instance, establishing a commission to provide financial advice to the industry. But the national commission provided no specific reason for its proposal nor any persuasive discussion of what benefits would accrue. Indeed, not only would a financial advisory commission be unlikely to have any meaningful policy leverage, it could actually foster collusion among airlines. The proposal should be ignored—as it apparently has been. Similarly, a fuel tax break for the industry, another recommendation, is subsidy and is not justifiable. There is no market imperfection that justifies such a tax break. A final recommendation, passing legislation that would prohibit permanently replacing striking workers, is also ill advised. It is better to allow the industry's labor-management relations to work themselves out in experiments at the different airlines. In general, taxes and regulations directed toward the industry should be justified on cost-benefit grounds.

Infrastructure

Given the industry's evolution, efficient pricing of and investments in airports and air traffic control—both long advocated by economists— take on added importance.[2] Efficient pricing amounts to charging aircraft

1. See National Commission to Ensure a Strong Competitive Airline Industry, *Change, Challenge and Competition* (Washington, 1993).

2. See, for example, Steven A. Morrison and Clifford Winston, "Enhancing the Performance of the Deregulated Air Transportation System," *Brooking Papers on Economic Activity: Microeconomics* (1989), pp. 61–123.

for their takeoffs and landings on airport runways according to the cost of the delay that each aircraft imposes on other aircraft. During peak travel times, when one plane can delay many others, the cost would be high; during off-peak periods the cost would be low, perhaps nothing. Current airport fees are based on aircraft weight and have nothing to do with delay costs. Efficient airport user fees should reduce delays from congestion by encouraging planes, especially general aviation and commuter planes, to use congested airports during off-peak periods or to switch to less congested airports. Efficient pricing would also eliminate the need for limitations on flight operations that are currently in effect at four high-density airports (Chicago O'Hare, New York Kennedy and LaGuardia, and Washington National).

Efficient airport investment calls for runway capacity to be expanded to the point that the marginal benefit of additional capacity, primarily in the form of less delay, equals the marginal cost of the capacity. Currently, the marginal benefit from an additional runway at most congested airports greatly exceeds its marginal cost.[3] To the extent feasible, congested airports should build more runways. By reducing congestion, efficient infrastructure policy will help airlines reduce operating costs and improve productivity. Indeed, Southwest has increased the efficiency of its aircraft use by avoiding congested airports wherever possible. Travelers, of course, will also benefit from less delay.

The air traffic control system must anticipate and be prepared to handle changes in air traffic patterns and flows resulting from domestic and international network restructuring. The Department of Transportation has advocated removing air traffic control from the Federal Aviation Administration and establishing it as an independent government corporation to make it more efficient and responsive to technological advances and changes in air travel. Well-defined interest groups, especially those who fly smaller planes and fear they will face higher landing and takeoff charges, oppose efficient infrastructure policy, especially congestion fees, and organizational changes in air traffic control. If the federal government truly wants to improve air transportation service and the carriers' financial performance, it must be committed to overcoming parochial interests in the pursuit of better infrastructure policy.

---

3. See Morrison and Winston, "Enhancing the Performance of the Deregulated Air Transportation System."

Open Skies

Although the federal government has in the past pursued a policy of open skies by trying to negotiate multilateral agreements that would allow unrestricted access to international airline markets, this approach to international airline competition has now been abandoned. The Clinton administration considers the current policy of negotiating bilateral agreements with individual countries the best that can be done. Whatever the path, however, the long-term goal should be clear: a fully deregulated international aviation environment in which any carrier can fly between any two countries it wishes and set its own fares.

In its negotiations and public relations with foreign governments, the U.S. government should stress the potential benefits of global deregulation for travelers throughout the world. Washington should insist on fully deregulated fare and market entry competition. That foreign carriers will acquire access to a larger market than U.S. carriers will should not be an overriding concern. Nor should foreign governments' subsidization of their carriers stand in the way of deregulation. Our isolated airline industry has become efficient and is ready to take on the world.

Conclusion

Although economists and other advocates of deregulation have a good track record in predicting its overall benefits, they have seriously underestimated the difficulty of the transition and the time it would take for the industry to adjust. Indeed, with its highly volatile financial performance and its leadership and structure constantly changing, the industry has obviously not reached long-run equilibrium. Still, most travelers and carriers have benefited from deregulation, and the industry is evolving in a direction that will preserve and may even enhance these benefits.

The evolution has been unsettling and has prompted calls for greater government intervention in the industry. But people's allegiance is forever vacillating between the free market and government regulation. When an industry is struggling, they say the government should help. When a government program falters, they call for market competition. So that we do not change our philosophy with every newspaper headline, it is important to have an objective empirical perspective.

The problems of the past few years should not fool Americans into thinking they are worse off or that the airline industry is fundamentally unsound. Airline deregulation was proposed and scrutinized for years before it was put into effect. The vision of greater public welfare springing from minimal government intervention in the air transportation market has been supported by events and by what one can see of the future.

Index

Bankruptcy and liquidation. *See* Airline industry; Airlines (tables); *individual major airlines*
Bannister, D., 4n
Barla, Philippe, 111n
Barnett, Donald F., 91
Baumol, William J., 40n, 43n
Berndt, Ernst R., 97, 98n
Bernheim, B. Douglas, 110n, 111n
Berry, Steven T., 131
Borenstein, Severin, 4n, 19n, 39n, 41n, 45n, 98n
Brander, James A., 87n
Brown, Walter, 3
Brueckner, Jan K., 39n
Button, K. J., 4n

CAB. *See* Civil Aeronautics Board
Call, Gregory D., 39n, 40n
Canada, 15, 147, 148
Card, David, 13n, 103n
Carlton, Dennis W., 23n
Causality. *See* Fares
Caves, Douglas W., 12
Civil Aeronautics Act of *1938*, 3
Civil Aeronautics Board (CAB), 4, 12, 62, 147. *See also* Mergers; Regulation and deregulation
Clinton administration, 162
Collusion, 68n, 110, 160
Commuter airlines, 32
Competition, 49; actual and potential, 39–40, 43n; airports and, 45, 73, 133; causality and, 73–75; deregulation and, 7, 8–9, 10–11, 18, 21n, 33, 149; frequent flier programs, 49–61; impediments, 33, 43–67, 159; international, 147–49; measurement, 9–11; price leadership and, 74–75; profitability and, 105; regulation and, 49; on routes, 73n; safety and, 31–32; smaller carriers, 61
Computer reservation systems (CRS), 33; biases, 61–67, 100, 102; booking fees, 65n, 96n, 100, 102; costs, 62–63, 100; deregulation and, 62–63, 104; hosts, 61n, 62, 100–101; rates of return, 100n, 102
Connecting flights: deregulation and, 27, 34–35; hub-and-spoke systems, 22–23; on-line and interline, 22–23, 34–35
Contestable markets theory, 43n
Continental Airlines: bankruptcies, 108, 145; competition, 71; fares, 71, 152n; losses, 30n; management, 101–02; market share, 59, 61

Costs and benefits: in bankruptcy, 106; causality and, 75–76, 77; computer reservation systems, 62–63, 100; connections, 34–35; deregulation and, 25–26, 62–63, 104, 149; fares, 17, 77–82, 143, 149n, 150–54; forecast errors, 91–96, 154; fuel, 13; input costs, 97; load factors, 25–26, 103–04; price–cost margins, 75–76, 86–88; price signaling, 77–78; rates of return, 99; reducing costs, 151; takeoff and landing, 41, 46, 160–61; traveler welfare costs, 77–82, 88–89; travel restrictions, 78–82; travel time and, 23–24. *See also* Fares; Labor
Crandall, Robert L., 71, 91
Crandall, Robert W., 91
CRS. *See* Computer reservation systems

Databases: computerized airfares, 67; Department of Transportation, 6n, 10n, 13, 17n, 23n, 41n, 69n, 129, 132n, 149, 151n
Daughety, Andrew F., 39n
Davidson, Joe, 67n, 78n
Delta Airlines: competition, 138, 143; enplanements, 7; fares, 72, 114, 143, 145; frequent flier program, 59; hubs, 20, 45n, 59, 72; international service, 148; management, 101–02; market share, 59, 61; multimarket contacts, 114; profits and losses, 109; routes, 128, 130
Department of Justice, 67, 77–78
Department of Transportation, 12. *See also* Databases
Deregulation. *See* Regulation and deregulation
De Vany, Arthur, 49n
Douglas, George W., 21n, 25n
Dyer, Nichola T., 39n

Eastern Airlines: bankruptcy and liquidation, 4, 10, 30, 90, 109, 145; fares, 72, 145; history, 3; management, 101–02
Economic issues: airline overcapacity, 91; airline profitability, 90, 92n, 96–105; business cycles, 153, 159; forecasting, 91–96, 104n, 153; gross domestic product (GDP), 92–95, 153n; *1990s* economic slowdown, 6, 10, 102n, 104n, 113; stockholder equity, 30; subsidies, 160, 162. *See also* Revenues
Edwards, Corwin D., 110n
Essential air service provision, 19n. *See also* Airline Deregulation Act of *1978*
European Union, 15, 148
Evans, William N., 39n, 111n, 113n